I0820117

Praise for *The Great Kosher Meat War of 1902: Immigrant Housewives and the Riots That Shook New York City* by Scott D. Seligman

2020–21 READER VIEWS LITERARY AWARD, GOLD MEDAL WINNER

2021 INDEPENDENT PUBLISHER BOOK AWARD, GOLD MEDAL WINNER

2020 NATIONAL JEWISH BOOK AWARD, FINALIST

"A highly readable and enjoyable account of this little-known episode in American history. Highly recommended, especially for those interested in American history and Jewish history, as well as gender and labor studies."

—*Library Journal*, starred review

"Seligman's compelling book is, first and foremost, a master class in historical storytelling. . . . A welcome contribution to Jewish historical literature that both general and academic readers would enjoy."

—Hannah Zaves-Greene, *American Jewish Archives Journal*

"A well-written narrative history, this will appeal to historians and social scientists as well as general readers interested in a powerful but little-known community action program."

—D. R. Jamieson, *Choice*

"Seligman writes easy-to-read prose, making this book perfect for scholars and non-scholars to appreciate his research. . . . . Anyone interested in life on the Lower East Side during the turn of the last century, Jewish women's history, or Jewish immigrant life will enjoy learning about this intriguing episode of Jewish American history."

—Rabbi Rachel Esserman, *Reporter*

"Seligman's well-researched book offers a valuable window into the emergence of direct-action protest among immigrant women on Manhattan's Lower East Side. In defending their families' interests, the women boycotters displayed a high degree of intelligence, boldness, and militancy that set a new standard for activism among working-class women."

—Gerald W. McFarland, *Criminal Law and Criminal Justice Books*

"A tale well worth remembering."

—Ira Wolfman, *Jewish Book Council*

"Highly readable. . . . [Seligman] succeeds in bringing to life the largely forgotten and primarily female leaders of the consumer campaign, their roles within the collective effort to bring down the prices of kosher beef, their internal divisions that developed, and their significance for American Jews. . . . [This book] provides vivid and intimate portrayals of the central actors who did the hard work of organizing a large-scale consumer boycott amid the relocation of nearly two million Jews to America. . . . An important contribution to the scholarship on the kosher meat boycott of 1902, as well as American Jewish women's history."

—Aaron Welt, Gotham Center for New York City History

"[Seligman] has done a service in bringing this little-known part of American history to our attention, one which demonstrates that the convergence of activism, socialism, and unionization prevalent in the early twentieth century remains a staple in protests to this day."

—Mike Maggio, *Washington Independent Review of Books*

"Seligman draws a splendid picture of life in the New World for these emigres from Poland, Lithuania, and the Pale of Russia. They formed associations, elected leaders, and in response to the increase in prices, led what they called 'strikes,' finding inspiration in the labor unions of the nineteenth century. Seligman uses as his primary resource the many Yiddish newspapers that were published daily. Each of those papers had its own take on the unrest that developed."

—Roger I. Abrams, *New York Journal of Books*

"Master storyteller Scott D. Seligman weaves together the disparate narratives of New York's 1902 kosher meat boycott, America's first and only chief rabbi, and the notorious Meat Trust. Deeply researched and engagingly written, *The Great Kosher Meat War of 1902* takes its delighted readers back in time to the teeming streets of the Lower East Side and the rough-and-tumble world of its immigrant Jews."

—Pamela S. Nadell, author of *America's Jewish Women: A History from Colonial Times to Today*

"The first blow-by-blow account of the kosher meat boycott of 1902 and the Jewish immigrant women who devised and promoted it. Anticipating both the consumer movement and contemporary Jewish women's activism, *The Great Kosher Meat War of 1902* shows how commerce, labor, food, and gender explosively combined at a tempestuous moment in the history of New York City."

—Jonathan D. Sarna, University Professor and Joseph H. and Belle R. Braun Professor of American Jewish History at Brandeis University and author of *American Judaism: A History*

"Why would a strike led by immigrant women in 1902 be important today? In this carefully crafted book, Scott D. Seligman drew from original *zaftik* (juicy) Yiddish news sources to bring to life the women brave enough to strike against their butchers. At the intersection of religion and politics, their cause gave rise to a mass movement not unlike those of today that pit human values against crass commercial interests."

—Miriam Isaacs, professor of Yiddish language and culture emerita, University of Maryland

"Scott D. Seligman has performed a bit of a miracle in letting the immigrant Jewish women who led the great meat boycott of 1902 find their voice today. Seligman shows how and why women publicly organized America's first consumer boycott. Launched from New York's Lower East Side to fight precipitous Chicago Beef Trust price hikes, their action spread to other cities, providing a powerful model for future activism."

—Elissa Sampson, visiting scholar and lecturer at Cornell University

The Great Christmas Boycott of 1906

The Great Christmas Boycott of 1906

ANTISEMITISM AND THE BATTLE OVER CHRISTIANITY IN THE PUBLIC SCHOOLS

SCOTT D. SELIGMAN

Potomac Books
An imprint of the University of Nebraska Press

 Potomac Books is an imprint
of the University of Nebraska Press.
Manufactured in the United States of America.

For customers in the EU with safety/GPSR concerns, contact:
gpsr@mare-nostrum.co.uk
Mare Nostrum Group BV
Mauritskade 21D
1091 GC Amsterdam
The Netherlands

Library of Congress Control Number: 2025015449

Designed and set in Arno Pro by K. Andresen.

Contents

Illustrations

Preface

Although now well into my seventies, I can still recite the twenty-third *and* twenty-fourth psalms I learned as a child. King James Version. Verbatim.

Even though the verses are from the Hebrew Bible, this Jewish boy certainly didn't learn those English translations in Hebrew School, where the teachers would never have ventured within a hundred yards of that Church of England version. The text was, rather, drilled into me, together with the distinctly *un*-Jewish Lord's Prayer, in public school in Newark, New Jersey, in the late 1950s and very early 1960s, by gentile and Jewish teachers alike. They had to. State law required it.

Before the recitation of the Pledge of Allegiance, which was also mandatory—"under God" and all—there was a Bible reading every morning, though never, in my memory, anything from the New Testament. Between the two was the Lord's Prayer, during which we were instructed to fold our hands and bow our heads, even though you'd never hear that prayer, which comes right out of the Gospels of Matthew and Luke, or see anyone pray in that posture, in a synagogue.

To the best of my recollection and those of several classmates with whom I am still in touch, we didn't have Christmas trees at Maple Avenue School, whose faculty and student body were so overwhelmingly Jewish at the time that the Board of Education could barely keep it open on the Jewish High Holy Days of Rosh Hashanah and Yom Kippur. We didn't sing carols other than innocuous ones like "Rudolph, the Red-Nosed Reindeer," which mentions Santa Claus, but not Jesus Christ. A non-Jewish classmate from back then reminds me that we may also have sung the "Dreidel Song." I trust her memory more than my own on that point, because she knows the lyrics, and she certainly didn't learn them at the Weequahic Presbyterian Church.

On the other hand, another gentile friend my age who grew up in nearby New Providence, where Jews were few, recalls singing "Come Thou Almighty King" in school and is sure there *was* a Christmas tree in *his* classroom. He remembers making decorations for it out of construction paper and library paste.

Friends who grew up across the Hudson River and are products of the New York City public school system have very different memories. None remembers Bible reading or Christmas songs, but several have vague memories of daily recitation of something called the Regents' Prayer, an ostensibly nondenominational appeal to God for blessings.

Why the difference? In the course of undertaking the research for this book, I learned that the states and even individual communities within them often went their separate ways on the controversial issue of what religion was and was not allowed in their public schools. I discovered that the seeds of such arrangements could be traced back to decisions made decades earlier by state legislatures, governors, courts, boards of education, and sometimes school principals. In the case of New York, an important factor was an event at the turn of the twentieth century, after its Jews, in newly swollen numbers, had their plea for secularism in the public schools fall on deaf ears. The citywide boycott they organized on the day of the school Christmas pageants in the year 1906, an act of civil disobedience little-remembered today, is the subject of this book.

I feel a need to confess at the outset that it has always seemed patently obvious to me that public schools are no place for Christmas trees *or* dreidels, much less nativity scenes, crucifixes, carols, menorahs, Islamic stars, or crescents. I understand that people have a right to free expression of religion, but to my mind, that's what houses of worship, parochial schools, and homes are for. Public schools are in a different category precisely because any organized devotional activities there risk putting the government's imprimatur on a particular brand of worship. I believed for years that I had the Establishment Clause of the Constitution—that part of the First Amendment that bars government from passing laws "respecting an establishment of religion"—squarely on my side on this point and I still do, even though many judicial opinions disagree and, in the eyes of some, the issue is not as black and white as it has always appeared to me.

As a practical matter, the Establishment Clause notwithstanding, religion has *never* been absent from public school classrooms in the United States and given the activism of the Christian right and the current makeup of the Supreme Court for which that faction is largely responsible, it isn't likely to disappear any time soon. At times it has been excluded—in 1980, for example, when the Supreme Court found a Kentucky law requiring the posting of the Ten Commandments in every public school classroom unconstitutional, as it had "no secular purpose" and was "plainly religious in nature." At other times it has been readmitted, such as the court's 2022 decision to permit a Washington state public school coach to hold prayers with his players at midfield after football games. The Roberts Court asserted that this had to be accepted as "part of learning how to live in a pluralistic society."

This waxing and waning testify to the fact that the line between the religious and the secular has never been a sharp one when it comes to the public schools, and that it has shifted from time to time, varied from state to state and community to community, sometimes been respected scrupulously and sometimes ignored entirely. Recent efforts by Christian nationalists to inject their religion into the nation's classrooms illustrate the staying power of the issue and the powerful divisions in American society that inevitably conspire to ensure that no rule seems ever to remain in place for long. That the matter continues to be the subject of passionate debate well into the twenty-first century not only proves that it has not been settled; it suggests that it probably never will be.

The controversy has been raging almost since the founding of the republic. This book tells the story of the entry of Jews into the dispute, which initially had been more or less an intramural Christian scrimmage pitting

Protestants against later-arriving Catholics. It is, appropriately, set in New York City, which in 1906 was home to the largest community of Jews in the United States—and, for that matter, the world.

This is a story of how Jewish activists first grumbled about Christmas celebrations in the public schools and eventually, viewing them as proselytizing efforts, decided to try to stop them. And how, when their voices were ignored, they raised the stakes. It tells how Jews and Christians did battle over the issue and how the American Jewish community was itself divided over whether to pursue it. It tells how the various communities consistently talked past one another—one side marshaling legal arguments, the other resorting, variously, to condescension, patriotism, racism, traditionalism, and outright dishonesty. And it tells how the Jewish community has itself changed and shifted focus in recent years, presumably after concluding that politics will probably never permit an unalloyed victory, much less a long-lasting one, and how, ironically, the passage of time has accomplished much of what the early Jewish activists could not.

Acknowledgments

First and foremost, let me express my appreciation to several distinguished scholars who gave generously of their time to review the manuscript that became this book and offer suggestions that made it an immeasurably better work:

- Dr. Jeffrey S. Gurock, Libby M. Klaperman Professor of Jewish History at the Bernard Revel Graduate School of Jewish Studies of Yeshiva University;
- Dr. Jonathan Sarna, University Professor and the Joseph H. & Belle R. Braun Professor of American Jewish History and Director of the Schusterman Center for Israel Studies at Brandeis University;
- Dr. Pamela Nadell, Patrick Clendenen Professor of Women's and Gender History and Director of the Jewish Studies Program at American University;
- Dr. Charles H. Lippy, Martin Distinguished Professor of Religious Studies Emeritus, University of Tennessee-Chattanooga; and
- Dr. Steven Levine, Senior Fellow, Chinese History and Politics and U.S.-China Relations, Emeritus, University of Montana

I am also especially grateful to Robert Boston, Senior Adviser at Americans United for Separation of Church and State and Editor Emeritus of *Church & State* magazine, and Steven M. Freeman, Senior Counsel and Director of Legacy for the Anti-Defamation League, both recognized authorities on church-state issues, for thoughts and suggestions that also helped improve the book.

Other friends and family members who delved into all or part of the manuscript and offered suggestions were Marsha Cohan, Rita Gotfried, Sharon A. Graham, Daniel Grossman, Steven Herman, Cecile Johnston, Elana Kieffer, Paul Kilmer, Joanne Z. Lasko, Beverley Barton Seaver, Charles J. Sheehan, Harvey Solomon, Deborah Strauss, Glenn Sugameli, and Suzanne Zunzer. My heartfelt thanks to all of them.

Thanks as well to my fellow septuagenarian friends and former classmates Ira Belkin, Luisa Foley, Barry Friedman, Jerold Glyn, Matthew Lieff, the late Jane Kalfus Maine, the late Marilyn Maines, Stephen Mallon, Harvey Mantel, Mark Sarver, Sara Sill, and Denise Summer, for sharing their recollections of religious practices (or lack thereof) in their elementary and high schools in the 1950s and early 1960s.

Much appreciation goes also to Miriam Isaacs, former Visiting Associate Professor of Yiddish Language and Culture at the University of Maryland, who served as my sherpa during a very enjoyable romp through the various Yiddish-language sources consulted in this work.

For help in gathering images and research materials, I would like to thank Abigail Bacon, Head of Public Services and Outreach, Hebrew Union College Libraries; Connie F. Beach-Sims, Archives Specialist, National Archives and Records Administration; Renée Carl; Kenneth Cobb, Assistant Commissioner at NYC Department of Records and Information Services; Katie Ehrlich, Reference Archivist, NYC Department of Records; Frank F. Harding; Caroline Hillkirk; Cassia Kisshauer, Reference Services Librarian, the Center for Jewish History; Moira McCudden, Student Researcher, Special Collections, College of Wooster; Denise D. Monbarren, Special Collections Librarian, College of Wooster; Joanna Rios, Records Manager, Columbia University Archives; Jocelyn Wilk, University Archivist, Columbia University Archives; and Havva Charm Zellner, Digital Librarian, Jewish Theological Seminary Library.

And finally, my thanks to my indefatigable literary agent, Peter W. Bernstein, to Amy Pattullo for an excellent job of copyediting, and to Taylor Gilreath, Kayla Moslander, Rebecca Jefferson, Tish Fobben, and their colleagues at the University of Nebraska Press for their continued support of my work.

Author's Note

In this book, as with all of my works of narrative nonfiction, nothing has been fictionalized. The characters really existed and the events really occurred at the times indicated. All quotes that appear between quotation marks or in block form were recorded at the time, though in a few instances I have condensed material or added italics to make for smoother reading. And no thoughts have been attributed to people who left no records of them, nor have feelings or motives been ascribed to them that were not made explicit by their words or actions.

The Yiddish and Hebrew terms in this work, with minor exceptions, are romanized according to the pronunciations favored by Lower East Side Litvak Jews—those whose families originated in present-day Lithuania, Belarus, Latvia, and northeastern Poland. In a few cases, these spellings may deviate from common, modern orthography.

SCOTT D. SELIGMAN
WASHINGTON DC

Dramatis Personae

Isaac Bildersee (1887–1952)	Assistant superintendent of schools responsible for nearly two dozen schools in Brooklyn from 1946 until his death.
William Sheafe Chase (1858–1940)	Rector of Brooklyn's Bedford Avenue Episcopal Church.
Bernard Drachman (1861–1945)	Rabbi of the Orthodox Park East Synagogue, or *Zichron Ephraim*, on New York's Upper East Side.
David Hummell Greer (1844–1919)	Protestant Episcopal bishop of New York from 1908 to 1919.
Frank Fountain Harding (1853–1925)	Principal of P.S. 144, an elementary school in Brownsville, Brooklyn, New York, in 1906.
Augusta "Gussie" Herbert (1891–?)	Fourteen-year-old schoolgirl, who objected to Principal Frank Harding's remarks about Jesus Christ during a school assembly.
Edward Herbert (1865–1915)	Attorney; father of Augusta Herbert.
Isidore Hirschfield (1869–1949)	Secretary and counsel to the Orthodox Union who represented accusers of Frank Harding before the Board of Education.

John Hughes (1797–1864)	Bishop of the Archdiocese of New York who lobbied for state support of Catholic schools.
Nathan S. Jonas (1868–1943)	Jewish banker who served on the New York City Board of Education and headed its Committee on Studies and Text-Books.
Joseph Krauskopf (1858–1923)	Rabbi at Reform Congregation *Keneseth Israel* of Philadelphia and president of the Central Conference of American Rabbis.
Albert Lucas (1859–1923)	Secretary of the Union of Orthodox Jewish Congregations of America and tireless advocate for Jewish causes.
Judah Leon Magnes (1877–1948)	Prominent Reform rabbi affiliated with Temple Emanu-El, who was publicly critical of the campaign to ban Christmas celebrations in the public schools.
William Henry Maxwell (1852–1920)	Superintendent of public schools in New York City from 1898 to 1917.
Henry Pereira Mendes (1852–1937)	Rabbi and president of the Union of Orthodox Jewish Congregations of the United States.
Baruch Miller (1872–1927)	Chairman of the District 39 School Committee in Brooklyn.
A. Emerson Palmer (1853–1925)	Secretary of the New York Board of Education from 1898 to 1923.
Julia Richman (1855–1912)	New York's first female district superintendent of schools.
Jacob A. Riis (1849–1914)	Social reformer, photojournalist, and founder of a Christian mission on New York's Lower East Side.
Samuel Schulman (1864–1955)	Prominent Reform rabbi affiliated with Temple Beth-El, who supported the protest against Christmas celebrations in the public schools.

Abraham Stern (1852–1927) Chairman of the Committee on Elementary Education of the New York City Board of Education.

Samuel Young (1779–1850) Secretary of state of New York from 1842 to 1845.

JEWISH NEWSPAPERS

American Hebrew Weekly English-language Jewish magazine published in New York City beginning in 1879. In 1903 it merged with the *Jewish Messenger.*

American Israelite English-language Reform Jewish weekly published in Cincinnati beginning in 1854.

Die Wahrheit Socialist Yiddish-language daily, whose name translates as "The Truth," published between 1905 and 1919.

Forverts Socialist Yiddish-language daily known in English as "The Forward," published in New York beginning in 1897.

Hebrew Standard Orthodox English language weekly published in New York between 1882 and 1922.

Jewish Messenger Weekly English-language Jewish magazine published in New York City beginning in 1857. In 1903, it merged with the *American Hebrew* to form the *American Hebrew and Jewish Messenger.*

Jewish Voice St. Louis–based weekly covering Jewish life in the city and the Midwest, published in English and Yiddish between 1888 and 1933.

Morgen Zhurnal Orthodox, Yiddish-language daily known in English as the "Jewish Morning Journal," published in New York from 1901 to 1971.

Reform Advocate	Reform Jewish weekly published in Chicago from 1891 to 1946.
Yidishes Tageblatt	Orthodox, Yiddish-language daily known in English as the "Jewish Daily News," published in New York from 1885 to 1928.

The Great Christmas Boycott of 1906

Prologue

Boys and Girls, Be Like Christ

It was December 1905, and Brooklyn was abuzz with yuletide spirit. The Sunshine Society was gearing up to provide Christmas trees for the poor children of the borough. Youngsters were whispering their wishes for presents into Santa's ear at the Berlin, "Broadway's Great Christmas Store," which lured parents with an offer of a free color picture book with every purchase. And the *Brooklyn Citizen* filled nearly a whole page in its "special Xmas number" with an inspirational message from the Rev. Dr. J. F. Carson of the Central Presbyterian Church heralding "The Coming of the King."[1]

P.S. 144, an elementary school on the western edge of Brooklyn's fast-growing Brownsville neighborhood, was, like most local public schools, preparing for the holiday. The school, which had opened its doors only the previous year, accommodated twenty-four hundred students of both sexes in classes up to and including the eighth grade.[2]

Like Brownsville itself, P.S. 144's student body was overwhelmingly Jewish. Beginning in the 1880s, when the construction of the Brooklyn Bridge made the borough more easily accessible from Manhattan, Brooklyn absorbed hordes of immigrant Jews, some eager to leave behind the stifling railroad flats of the Lower East Side's teeming tenements, others fresh off the boat from Russia, Poland, Romania, Lithuania, Hungary, or elsewhere in Eastern Europe. This flow was accelerated by the opening of the Williamsburg Bridge in 1903. In the first years of the twentieth century, as many businesses opened in Brooklyn and began hiring, thousands more Jewish families relocated to Brownsville, whose population grew to sixty thousand by 1904.[3]

The vast majority of these immigrants enrolled their children in the public schools, which, to many Jewish parents, were a dream come true. They were free, they did not discriminate, and they offered a quick ticket to mastering English and learning American customs, and hence to advancing in society, something that had been nearly impossible in their former countries. And unlike money, jewelry, and property, education was an asset that could not be taken away.

This huge influx created a crush of too many students chasing too few desks and made it difficult for the city government to keep pace with school construction. Struggling to keep up, New York's Board of Education opened nine new elementary schools in Brooklyn alone in 1901–2, three more in 1902–3, and another four in 1904–5, to say nothing of existing school buildings that underwent expansion. This rapid development also created jobs and offered faculty and administrators already in the school system opportunities for rapid advancement. When P.S. 144 opened its doors in 1904, Frank Fountain Harding, since 1895 the principal of the far smaller P.S. 83, was tapped to take its helm.[4]

Gaunt, full-bearded, and balding, with what hair remaining combed back in long, flowing locks, Harding had been born in New York fifty-two years earlier. He had studied for his bachelor's degree at Columbia University's School of Political Science, married in 1885, and earned his doctorate at Ohio's College of Wooster in 1893. Afterward, he had accepted a job as a math teacher in a Chicago high school. By the middle of the decade, however, he had returned to his native Brooklyn and taken a position as a math teacher at the Manual Training High School on Seventh Avenue.

Harding had spent his entire career as an educator and was, by all accounts, a dedicated professional who took his responsibilities seriously. Something of a public figure, he lectured on the teaching of mathematics at the Brooklyn Institute of Arts and Sciences, preaching that problem solving improves a student's understanding and judgment. He gave generously of his time, even to support extracurricular activities. Harding recruited boys to join the American Guard of Cadets, a military-style regiment over which he presided as colonel, confident that "the school drill teaches the boys self-reliance, self-respect and betters them physically." He had also overseen the establishment of a free circulating library at P.S. 83 and donated a number of his own books to get it started.[5]

Raised in the Presbyterian church, Frank Harding also believed deeply in the redemptive power of Jesus Christ and thought his savior's message of truth and love would be beneficial to those who might not have heard it. So in 1905, with Christmas just around the corner, he took advantage of a December 19 assembly in the school auditorium to pass it along to his charges.

Celebrating Christmas in the public schools was de rigueur in New York in 1905. A Christmas pageant on the day before the winter recess began was customary. On the very day of Harding's address, students at P.S. 64, just over a mile away, were rehearsing for their annual fête, which included the singing of "Christmas Bells," "Our Christmas Tree," and recitations of "A Tale of Christmas Postponed." In many schools, the programs included as many patriotic songs as they did religious ones, as celebrating the holiday was often conflated with being free and American. Even as early as the turn of the twentieth century, many saw it as more of a cultural event than a religious festival.

All this occurred annually despite the fact that New York's Jewish community had been growing exponentially; by 1905 it had reached nearly a million, accounting for some twenty percent of the city's overall population. Nobody seemed to view this as much of an issue, however. In fact, the *Brooklyn Daily Eagle* reported giddily about how much kindergarten and high school students of *all* persuasions enjoyed the "thoughts of Santa Claus, Christmas trees and presents surging through their brains."[6]

Harding began the assembly by reading aloud from a book entitled *Gems of Wisdom from Bible Literature and Proverbs*, a collection of quotations from Scripture. Its author, William J. Shearer, a fellow educator, claimed to have made a special effort to omit Bible verses that Catholics, Jews, and other non-Protestants might find offensive and to include only those to which "no reasonable objection can be made." But it wasn't much of an effort. He had filled its pages with dozens of verses from the King James edition of the New Testament, a translation rejected wholesale by Catholics, and an entire volume abhorred by Jews. The book even included a passage from the book of Acts that painted an unpleasant picture of blasphemous Jews jealously tearing into St. Paul.[7]

"Now boys and girls," Harding announced from the dais after the reading, "at this time of the year I want you all to have the feeling of Christ in you. Have more pleasure in giving than in taking. Be like Christ; that is how I want you to be. Christ blesses all but the hypocrites, and the hypocrites are the people who do not believe in him. He forgives all but those, so, boys and girls, be like Christ."[8]

These remarks did not sit well with fourteen-year-old Augusta Herbert, known as Gussie, a seventh grader among the five hundred pupils in the assembly. The plucky, New York–born daughter of Romanian immigrants, who was observant and well-schooled in her Jewish heritage, didn't feel like a hypocrite, and didn't appreciate the implication that she might be one. So, she screwed up her courage and advanced to the front of the auditorium to challenge her principal. She wanted to understand why he thought it proper to teach the Christian religion in a public school.

In a firm but muted voice that could nonetheless be heard clearly throughout the hall, she asked, pointedly but not impolitely, "Mr. Harding, don't you think that preaching on Christ belongs to the Sunday school or church and not to a public school?"[9]

"I'm not preaching by any means," she recalled him saying in response. And then, immediately contradicting himself, he added, "Anybody whom preaching on Christ does *not* suit may have the pleasure of leaving the room at any time." Then he ordered her back to her seat.[10]

Harding ought to have known better. He had received a letter from a parent just a week earlier admonishing him to avoid just this sort of injection of religion into school activities. He would soon have reason to regret not taking the warning to heart.

1

This Private, Clandestine, Surreptitious "Union of Church and State"

The history of free, publicly funded schools in New York City began exactly a century before Gussie Herbert rose to confront her principal for proselytizing, and religion had always been a central issue in it. In the eighteenth century, the city's schools had all been privately run under the aegis of churches or charitable organizations. Some charged parents a fee for educating their youngsters; others, supported by private philanthropy, were free to the children of the poor. Apart from teaching reading, writing, and arithmetic, all sought to inculcate moral and religious values. These, of course, varied, depending on whether the school had been organized, variously, by Baptists, Lutherans, Methodists, Presbyterians, Episcopalians, Quakers, Roman Catholics, or Jews.

Under this system, many poor, nonreligious children were left out, and to remedy this, a Free School Society was established by a group of citizens in 1805 at the urging of Mayor DeWitt Clinton. Its charge was to provide a basic education to white children whose families were not affiliated with any denomination (a privately funded school for African American students had been in operation since 1787). Although the State of New York approved the incorporation of the new organization, it did not initially offer it any financial support, so the work of the Free School Society had to be underwritten by contributions and dues. The body began by opening a weekday free school and a Sunday school for those unable to attend during the week.

The society was not attached to any particular sect, but religion was never far from the minds of its trustees, most of whom were Protestant. One of their stated goals was to "inculcate the sublime truths of religion and morality contained in the Holy Scriptures." They aimed to provide the children the society served with an ostensibly nondenominational, but actually unmistakably Protestant, education.[1]

By 1807 the Free School Society had begun to receive funding from the state legislature, and by 1822 it was running four schools that served more than two thousand students. But when, that same year, a local Baptist church sought financial support for its own school for poor children not necessarily of the Baptist faith and managed to get the state legislature to place it on a similar footing with the society, the trustees became alarmed and began a campaign to prevent religious organizations as a class from receiving state funds. They lobbied the legislature, which in 1824 washed its hands of the matter by delegating the right to choose local grantees to the Common Council of the City of New York.

The Free School Society then pushed the Common Council to cut church schools off from public moneys, which it did the following year. This meant that apart from minor grants to orphanages and a handful of other schools, the society received *all* the state funds. Although this move was potentially detrimental to all local sects, it was Catholics who felt the discrimination most acutely.

The Catholic population had begun to swell during the 1830s and 1840s due to explosive immigration from Ireland and Germany. But many Catholic parents in New York City did not wish to entrust their children to the schools run by the Free School Society—renamed the Public School Society in 1826—because these were perceived as anti-Catholic in outlook. They feared their children would be indoctrinated with teachings antithetical to those of their own church. So, in 1840, when William H. Seward, then governor of New York, proposed that immigrant children in state-funded schools be taught by "teachers speaking the same language with themselves, and professing the same faith," local Catholics saw an opening.[2]

Seward's move was arguably motivated as much by a desire to win the votes of Catholics, who now accounted for one-fifth of New York City's

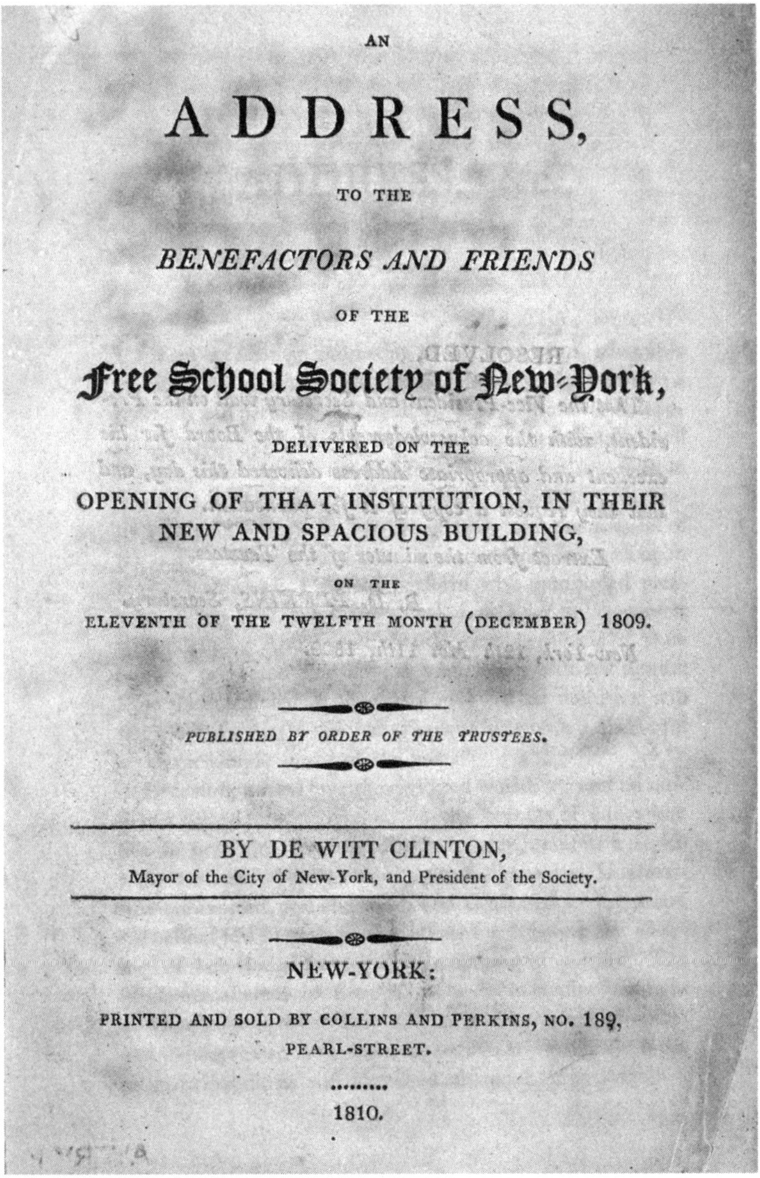

AN

ADDRESS,

TO THE

BENEFACTORS AND FRIENDS

OF THE

Free School Society of New-York,

DELIVERED ON THE

OPENING OF THAT INSTITUTION, IN THEIR
NEW AND SPACIOUS BUILDING,

ON THE

ELEVENTH OF THE TWELFTH MONTH (DECEMBER) 1809.

PUBLISHED BY ORDER OF THE TRUSTEES.

BY DE WITT CLINTON,
Mayor of the City of New-York, and President of the Society.

NEW-YORK:

PRINTED AND SOLD BY COLLINS AND PERKINS, NO. 189,
PEARL-STREET.

....

1810.

Fig. 1. Title page of a reprint of a December 1809 address by New York mayor DeWitt Clinton at the dedication of a new building for the Free School Society, an organization formed at his urging. DeWitt Clinton, Internet Archive (New York: Collins and Perkins, 1810), https://archive.org/details/ldpd_11290338_000.

population, as by a genuine concern for improving public education. It had been prompted by his good friend, Irish-born Bishop John Joseph Hughes, the nationally prominent coadjutor of the Roman Catholic Diocese of New York, who wished to gain state support for Catholic-run schools. In the fall of 1840, under Bishop Hughes's direction, the trustees of several Roman Catholic schools in New York City petitioned the Common Council for a portion of the school fund.[3]

Among the arguments they presented in their lengthy appeal:

- The books and general tone of instruction in Public School Society–run schools were strongly biased in favor of Protestantism. The school day was opened with a reading from the King James Bible, which differed substantially from the Catholic Scriptures. And many textbooks contained matter "prejudicial to the Catholic name and character."
- Because of this, Catholics had had no choice but to establish their *own* schools, and eight such institutions already existed in the city. This meant that local Catholics were paying taxes to support public schools *and* shouldering the expense of schools of their own. They were, in essence, being taxed twice.
- Although the Public School Society contended that state law disqualified religious schools from receiving public funds, in fact it did not. The state legislature had merely delegated such decisions to the city's Common Council.[4]
- Any government funds dispensed to Catholic schools would be used to support the teaching of the basic secular curriculum and not religious studies.

The Catholic petition was naturally opposed by the Public School Society, and a heated debate played out in the newspapers and in public meetings. Bishop Hughes delivered an eloquent speech before the Common Council and followed it up with several letters to the newspapers. He did not pull his punches. "It is this private, clandestine, surreptitious 'union of Church and State' against which Catholics have protested," he asserted. "It is this which has driven us from the public schools." He also made it clear that no reforms

Fig. 2. Bishop John Joseph Hughes, coadjutor of the Roman Catholic Diocese of New York, who is remembered as the father of Catholic education in America for his efforts to establish a network of Catholic parochial schools. Wikimedia Commons, upload.wikimedia.org/wikipedia/commons/c/ce/John_Hughes_archbishop_-_Brady-Handy.jpg.

the Public School Society might conceivably make in its schools would be satisfactory to Roman Catholics.[5]

The Public School Society trustees argued that their curriculum was essentially a secular one to which Catholics "could not reasonably object." They also raised the specter of all the Protestant denominations lining up to demand similar support should the Catholics be granted their request. And by a nearly unanimous vote, the Common Council denied the Catholic appeal.[6]

Undeterred, Bishop Hughes—known as "Dagger John" as much for his contentious, aggressive style as for the cross he appended to his signature—continued his agitation by lobbying the state legislature to overrule the Common Council. After extensive debate, a bill narrowly passed the legislature in 1842 that placed public education throughout the state into the hands of elected ward commissioners, supervised by a local board of education empowered to set standards. In a single stroke, it destroyed the Public School Society's monopoly, and within a decade the organization was gone. Bishop Hughes had won *that* battle. But he was unsuccessful in achieving his main objective, which was to secure state funding for the Catholic schools. The final bill banned sectarian teaching in publicly funded schools, foiling his grand plans for public support.[7]

Seeing no immediate prospect of government funding, Hughes launched a full-throttle initiative to establish a network of Catholic parochial schools. He pursued this effort single-mindedly until his death in 1864, and for this reason is remembered as the father of Catholic education in America.[8]

In 1842, attorney Samuel Young was appointed Secretary of the State of New York, which made him *ex officio* Superintendent of Common Schools. Because state law made no reference to the Bible, he wasted no time in declaring the New Testament "in all respects a suitable book to be daily read in our common schools." Praising both its literary and moral merit, he recommended its general acceptance for this purpose. To Young's mind, the Holy Bible was not a sectarian work and was hence a completely appropriate volume for use in publicly funded schools.

The freedom to make such decisions locally meant that some local school authorities could choose *not* to read the Bible, however, or at least not the King James Version. This happened in some predominantly Catholic districts of New York City, where local authorities either dispensed with Bible reading entirely or substituted the Douay Rheims Bible, the standard English-language Catholic Bible, which differed not only in translation but, to a certain extent, in content from Protestant bibles. This, in turn, led some to fear that Catholics might attempt to get the Board of Education to ban the King James Bible from the schools entirely. Such a rumor, spread widely in Philadelphia, led to a series of nativist, anti-Catholic riots in 1844 that resulted in the destruction of two Catholic churches in that city.

To guard against a similar uprising, the State of New York amended its school law to expressly *deny* to local boards of education the power to exclude the Bible. That same year, the New York City Board of Education ruled that the reading of the Bible, as long as it was not accompanied by note or comment, did not constitute sectarianism. And that remained the board's position into the twentieth century.[9]

Even at this early stage, Jews were not silent on religion in the public schools; they just lacked the numbers and the clout to make much of an issue of it. In 1842, immediately after Young declared his admiration for the New Testament, an anonymous Jewish resident of New York City wrote him predicting that his order would drive Jewish children from the schools. Young responded by pointing out that it was a *recommendation* rather than an order, "submitted to the judgment, the discretion, and the conscience of those who have the selection of books for district schools." This was probably cold comfort to the letter writer, however, since Jews, who numbered only about twenty thousand in the entire country at this stage, surely had little or no representation among the district officers whose judgment actually mattered.[10]

Occasional Jewish complaints did register with the authorities even at that early stage, but that did not necessarily mean any action was taken on them. An 1843 report from a select committee appointed by the newly established New York Board of Education reveals that Catholics, Universalists, and Jews had all objected to some books used in the schools of the city's fourth ward—the lower Manhattan neighborhood bordering on the East River. Catholics had protested the use of the King James Bible; Universalists, who rejected the concept of eternal damnation, objected to references to punishments in the afterlife. Jewish complaints generally centered on New Testament–related passages in three books, including one entitled *Lessons for Schools Taken from the Holy Scriptures*, which taught, among other things, that "the Son of God came from Heaven to save an erring world."

The trustees in charge of the fourth ward schools thought the Jews had a point and called for some of the books to be excluded. But this view was dismissed wholesale by the select committee, which found itself "unable to discover any possible ground of objection even by the Jews" except that they "inculcate the general principles of Christianity."

The Jews had no right to object to this, the committee reasoned, because they were latecomers. "The Jews have not, and from the very nature of our systems, cannot have the same privileges as those who embrace the Christian religion," it asserted. "In offering civil and religious liberty to the oppressed of other nations, it surely was not intended to give them the right of changing or interfering with our own religious institutions," adding that "your committee do not perceive that they have any just grounds of complaint, or that they can reasonably ask that such institutions should be changed for their convenience." The full board concurred and took no action on the complaints.[11]

A decade later, Isaac Mayer Wise, the well-known Reform rabbi, attacked sectarianism in the schools. Wise, who was at the time chaplain of the New York State Legislature—thanks, ironically, to the efforts of William H. Seward, now a U.S. Senator—wrote that "if anything like sectarian religion is taught in the public schools, the Israelites should complain and the school board is bound in duty to hear and redress the wrong."[12]

There was an effort in the Congress to amend the U.S. Constitution to prohibit tax money from being channeled to any religious school in the country. Such a bill was introduced in 1875 by Maine Representative James G. Blaine at the urging of President Ulysses S. Grant, primarily as a means of denying aid to Catholic schools. It passed the House of Representatives easily but failed to achieve the required two-thirds vote in the Senate. By that time, however, most states had already incorporated similar provisions into their individual constitutions.[13]

The waning years of the nineteenth century saw new laws mandating compulsory school attendance; a broadening of curricula to include subjects like science, music, and history; the institution of examinations to assess skills and knowledge; the development of normal schools to train teachers; and the end of segregated "colored schools" in New York State. With huge numbers of immigrants swelling the rolls, especially in New York City, these years also saw massive construction of new schools.

They also witnessed a growing paternalistic impulse on the part of members of the establishment to take it upon themselves to Americanize the mostly non–English speaking newcomers, whom many regarded as inferior, undesirable, immoral, clannish, unhygienic, and even threatening. There was only so much that public lectures and evening classes could do to mold uneducated, European-born adults into true Americans. But their children, if reached early, were another matter entirely. Through their teachers and principals in the public schools, they could be thoroughly inculcated with American values. To the *New York Tribune*, the schools were "the great citizen manufactory for these incoming foreigners."[14]

American values generally meant Protestant values, however, which, after all, had undergirded a good deal of what it had meant to be American for most of the country's history. Public schools were seen as centers of moral instruction as much as they were vehicles for the teaching of secular subjects like reading and writing, and to the extent that these favored Protestant interpretations, Catholics would never cease their objections to them and would continue to push for state aid for their own growing system of parochial schools.[15]

An 1889 survey by the Presbyterian Synod of New York gives a picture of the mixed bag that characterized the status of religion in the state's public schools at the turn of the century. Superintendents of schools in twenty-five cities, 114 commissioners of county schools, and a handful of others were sent questionnaires to which the majority replied. Of the city school districts that responded, fourteen mandated daily Bible readings while five forbade them, and six required the daily singing of Christian hymns. Instruction in morality was required in sixteen cities; in Rochester, this involved "all the Christian virtues and reverence for God." There was no such requirement, however, in Cohoes, Hudson, Newberg, Schenectady, or Troy. The county commissioners reported that twenty-four required moral instruction, whereas thirty-six did not.

In reporting about the survey, the *American Hebrew* agreed that morality should be taught. "Morals can only be taught by recognizing the religious sanction which gives morality its authority," it declared. But it quickly added that "we fear . . . that the Presbyterian gentlemen who are so active in this matter seek to substitute Christianity for Religion as the subject to be taught in the schools," and argued that doing so would "endanger the success of the cause we both have at heart." The paper's solution was to limit such instruction to the Old Testament, on which the two faiths might agree.[16]

When the various boroughs were consolidated into the City of Greater New York at the end of the nineteenth century, ostensibly to improve efficiency and cement New York's status as the nation's undisputed economic and cultural capital, a new city charter was drafted. It reiterated the provision that the Board of Education had no power to exclude the Bible from the public schools. But it also included the words "no school shall be entitled to receive any portion of the school monies in which the religious doctrines or tenets of any particular Christian or other religious sect shall be taught, implicated or practiced."[17]

As Jews—who, unlike many Catholics, revered the public schools and largely *preferred* to send their children to them—were poised to join the debate in a big way, their principal goal was simply to hold the powers-that-be to that very pledge.[18]

2

Those Ever-Watchful Collectors of Stray Lambs

Full-bearded and silver-haired, Albert Lucas had an oval face, a high forehead, blue-gray eyes, and a light complexion, and was most often seen balancing a pair of bifocal pince-nez spectacles precariously on the bridge of his nose. He liked to think he bore some resemblance to King Edward VII, and he actually did, though he was quite a bit shorter than the monarch. Although he stood only five feet three inches tall, his diminutive stature had never been an impediment to being taken seriously.

Born Abraham Abrahamson in Liverpool in 1859, the son of a watchmaker, he came from a long line of Dutch Jews. Lucas attended the City of London School, an endowed, independent boys' day school established by a private Act of Parliament that offered a progressive curriculum and—most importantly—did not discriminate on the basis of religious persuasion. This meant that unlike many other academies of the time, it was open to Jewish students.[1]

An accomplished debater who once interned in a British solicitor's office, Lucas boasted in later life of having taken on British political activist Charles Bradlaugh, an avowed atheist who went on to serve in Parliament, and Annie Besant, a well-known socialist, theosophist, and women's rights activist with a reputation as a brilliant orator. From childhood, he never shrank from an argument or a conflict. A scrappy man of strong convictions, he was scrupulously honest and never shy about expressing his opinions forcefully and publicly.

Lucas had studied Hebrew with a Sephardic teacher in London and gravitated to Sephardic congregations throughout his life. An observant, Orthodox Jew, he emigrated to the United States in 1888 and married two years later. His wife, Rebecca Nieto, three years his junior and, like him, British-born, was Sephardic royalty. She was a lineal descendant of Venetian-born Rabbi David Nieto, a physician, theologian, mathematician, poet, and author prominent in London's Spanish and Portuguese Jewish community in the early eighteenth century.[2]

Rebecca's father, British-born Abraham Haim Nieto, was also a rabbi. After spending fourteen years in Jamaica, he had joined New York's Spanish and Portuguese synagogue, Shearith Israel, North America's very first Jewish congregation. It was he who officiated at the marriage of his daughter to Lucas on December 24, 1890. The wedding was a lavish affair with Nathans, Blumenthals, Lazaruses, Phillipses, Kursheedts, and other prominent members of New York's German and Sephardic Jewish elite in attendance. Lucas remained a member of Shearith Israel for the rest of his life.[3]

After spending a few years on Staten Island, where he founded a local Hebrew benevolent society and a religious school, he became a naturalized American citizen in 1896 and moved with his wife to Manhattan two years later. There he worked with Episcopal Bishop Henry Codman Potter, a prominent social reformer, as a volunteer investigator of conditions on the Lower East Side, where most of New York's recent Jewish immigrants lived. Unlike the earlier-arriving German and Sephardic Jews, many of whom had prospered since their immigration and moved uptown, these "downtown Jews" were principally Yiddish-speaking Ashkenazis from Russia and Central Europe, and they made up the vast majority of New York's Jewish community. Most were observant and many were desperately poor.[4]

Although he derived his income as an importer of specialty groceries, Lucas was most passionate about his faith. He worked tirelessly to promote traditional Judaism, make America safe for Jews to practice their religion, promote the welfare of Jews of all stripes, and oppose all forms of antisemitism. The *Hebrew Standard* once wrote that his motto was "don't talk so much—*do* something," but in fact he did a great deal of both. In the early years of the twentieth century until his untimely death in 1923, Albert Lucas was a veritable Jewish whirling dervish as he toiled tirelessly to advance all of these causes.[5]

Lucas was deeply opposed to the growing Reform movement, which he believed was luring Jewish youth away from orthodoxy and, in so doing, threatening the very future of Judaism in America. As early as 1897, he began to speak out against the thousands of Jews in New York he believed had "no religion or faith" despite being members of Reform temples, and was especially critical of those who failed to observe the Sabbath. He made common cause with others who felt, as he did, the need to beat back the steady advances Reform had made in the closing decades of the nineteenth century.[6]

When, in 1898, Shearith Israel's Rabbi Henry Pereira Mendes, another British-born Sephardi from a prominent rabbinical family, joined with representatives of several dozen synagogues to establish the Union of Orthodox Jewish Congregations of America, Lucas, a masterful writer, was chosen as a secretary of the new organization. Its chief goals were to defend traditional Judaism against all threats and, explicitly, to oppose "the declarations of Reform rabbis not in accord with our Torah."[7]

The Orthodox Union, as it became known, spoke out on many issues. It pushed the federal government to deploy Jewish chaplains in the armed services and offer furloughs to Jewish soldiers on the High Holy Days. It sent lists of Jewish holidays to the presidents of colleges and universities and to organizations like the State Board of Medical Examiners, asking that no examinations be given on those days so Jewish students might be free to worship. It opposed "Sunday laws" that forbade everyone—Jews included—from doing business on the Christian Sabbath. It fought against changes to immigration law that would have hindered the coming of Russian and European Jews fleeing persecution. It railed against Reform congregations that had begun to follow Christian practice by celebrating the Sabbath on Sundays. And it complained about Jews who intermarried with gentiles, as well as those who contented themselves with civil divorces and did not seek religiously sanctioned ones as well.[8]

Lucas's was one of the Orthodox Union's loudest voices, and he did not waste any time before taking on one of the city's most prominent critics of the Jews, attorney Frank Moss. An antivice crusader, Moss had been associated with many reform movements in the city and in 1897 had succeeded Theodore Roosevelt as president of the city's Board of Police Commissioners. Moss had just published a three-volume work entitled *The American Metropolis from Knickerbocker Days to the Present Time* in which he castigated Jewish immigrants for "ignorance, prejudice, stubborn refusal to yield to American ideas, religious habits and requirements, clannishness and hatred and distrust of Christians," and decried the "criminal instincts that are so often found naturally in the Russian and Polish Jews."[9]

Responding in the *Hebrew Standard* to a glowing review of Moss's book that appeared in the *New York Herald*, a paper widely known for its anti-Jewish views, Lucas demolished Moss's arguments one by one, accused him of "groping in the mire," and turned his own language back on him, arguing that "ignorance, prejudice, stubborn refusal to see anything good in a people he hates renders his criticism valueless to the thoughtful."[10]

Initially, the Orthodox Union was something of an elitist body. Its organizers were largely Western-educated, English-speaking, uptown Jews of Sephardic, German, or English extraction. They focused much of their energy, however, on their less fortunate but far more numerous downtown brethren. They worried that many of the downtowners were becoming less religious in the freer atmosphere of New York than they had been in their old countries. And that their American-born children were alarmingly ignorant of Judaism and its traditions.

Jewish education for children was available, generally through *Talmud Torahs*, which held after-school classes where the basics of the religion were taught, or from roving tutors engaged by parents to drill their sons for some ten cents a week. But beyond, perhaps, the Hebrew alphabet, excerpts from the Hebrew Bible, and a few frequently recited prayers, few had much formal knowledge of Jewish beliefs, Jewish law, or Jewish history.[11]

"Downtown we have a fertile field of children living in an atmosphere that is *quasi*-Jewish," Lucas wrote of this alarming state of affairs. "It is not a healthy Jewish atmosphere." But he did not believe the situation was beyond repair. It was out of this conviction that he more or less singlehandedly established a network of religious classes in downtown synagogues to teach Jewish boys and girls about their heritage.[12]

With very little in the way of resources, Lucas began the program in 1900 with a class at the Pike Street Synagogue—*B'nai Israel Kalwaria*. He did not ask the congregation for financial support, only for the use of its facilities. The effort was successful, so he expanded it to several other East Side *shuls* (synagogues) willing to make space available, and he opened his classes to girls as well as boys. Lucas, who didn't speak Yiddish, recruited volunteers who did; he himself taught some of the classes in English. All served without compensation. In addition to instruction in Hebrew and Bible history, the program included celebrations of Jewish holidays, discussions of the weekly Torah readings, songfests, field trips, and lectures. The lessons became so closely associated with him that they came to be known as the Albert Lucas Religion Classes. By 1905, some thirty volunteer teachers were holding classes for about seven hundred Jewish students. The lessons continued for many years and educated thousands of Jewish children, some of whom later signed on as teachers themselves.[13]

Lack of a Jewish education was a threat, but it was something Jews could remedy themselves through programs like the Lucas classes. A second, external challenge that was also alienating Jewish children from their traditions was less easily addressed. Efforts by Christian missionaries, through their settlement houses, to bring Jewish children to Jesus, were also of grave concern, and in the early years of the twentieth century, the Orthodox Union began to focus its energies on addressing this peril.

Lucas laid it all out in an incendiary paper he delivered in June 1903 before the third annual convention of the Orthodox Union. He decried "those ever-watchful collectors of stray lambs who conduct kindergartens and such like institutions, to which the children of the poor are always welcome—most welcome if they happen to be of Jewish parentage." Noting that the walls of these places were decorated with pictures of Jesus Christ performing charitable acts, he concluded that their whole object was "to instill into the minds of the infants a feeling of love for a faith different to that of their parents."

He acknowledged that the basic problem stemmed in large part from the failure of East Side parents to educate their children in the Jewish faith and conceded that the simplest solution would be for Jewish families to keep their children away from such places. But this was easier said than done, because

Fig. 3. Albert Lucas, secretary of the Union of Orthodox Jewish Congregations of America, who worked tirelessly to promote traditional Judaism and make America safe for Jews to practice their religion. American Jewish Historical Society, *The Joint Distribution Committee Album, 1914–1954* (New York: American Jewish Joint Distribution Committee, 1954).

the settlement houses provided services like meals, health care, education, childcare, and job placement that poor families needed. He was especially critical of the deceptive methods used by some of them—such as serving matzoh during Passover and preparing special Purim treats—to mislead suspicious or inquisitive parents into believing that Jewish traditions were actually being honored.[14]

The following August, the crusade against settlement houses got personal. The Danish-American Jacob A. Riis, a well-known and highly respected champion of the poor and oppressed and an apostle of Americanization, suddenly came in for withering criticism for surreptitious proselytizing.

At first blush, Riis was an improbable target. In the text and the images in *How the Other Half Lives,* his popular, pioneering work of photojournalism first published in 1890, he had cast a revealing light on the desperate poverty endured by New York's immigrants, including its Jews. He was an advocate of safer tenements and more playgrounds and an opponent of corruption in government—all causes the Jewish community supported. His Henry Street settlement house—which he established in 1890 with the Circle of the King's Daughters, an organization of Episcopal women—was highly

Fig. 4. Jacob A. Riis, Danish-American social reformer and photojournalist who drew attention to the plight of New York's impoverished but who was criticized for using his Lower East Side settlement house to convert Jewish children to Christianity. Library of Congress, LC-USZ62–57745. Photo by Pirie McDonald.

praised for its good works and had been renamed "The Jacob Riis House" in his honor a decade later. Even the Jewish press had generally covered his writings favorably and quoted his lectures, which were sometimes delivered in synagogues.

So it must have seemed to many a bolt out of the blue when suddenly, in mid-August 1903, the *American Hebrew and Jewish Messenger* ran a column entitled "A Voice from the Ghetto" accusing Riis of "thinly covered missionary endeavors." It actually should not have been a surprise; Riis had hinted at his ambitions to proselytize quite early on. In an 1893 essay in *The Independent* entitled "The Heathen of New York," he had written approvingly of the opportunity to bring the sixty thousand children in "Jewtown" to Jesus, noting that even their own rabbis fretted about "the visible falling away of the young." Here Riis saw possibilities. He predicted that "we shall shortly have a colony of infidels over on the East Side, the responsibility for which will be ours."[15]

In his various writings, Riis had expressed admiration for the Jewish people about as often as he had condemned them. On one point, however, he was consistent: despite their many positive attributes, he believed Jews

Fig. 5. The Jacob A. Riis Neighborhood Settlement at 48–50 Henry Street, Manhattan. Library of Congress, Manuscript Division, Jacob A. Riis Papers, *Twenty-Eighth Annual Report, 1917–1918*, page 2.

sadly in error when it came to their beliefs. "In all matters pertaining to their religious life," he wrote in *How the Other Half Lives*, "they stand, these East Side Jews . . . stubbornly refusing to see the light."[16]

No one had made much of an issue of these statements at the time, perhaps because Riis was so highly regarded or because he was such a strong advocate of many causes local Jews also supported. But that changed in 1903. Without mentioning Riis by name, but leaving no doubt that it was *his* mission house that was the subject of the *American Hebrew* column, its author—a regular contributor to the publication who identified himself only as "One of the Submerged"—reported rumors that Jewish children had returned to their homes from his settlement house singing hymns about Jesus Christ and the Virgin Mary, to the horror of their parents.

The author had apparently queried Riis directly about this, because he quoted the Dane's combative response: "Yes, the house is a Christian Settlement, and it is going to remain that. We have nailed the cross to the door, and it is going to remain there. If your Jewish mothers don't know where they are sending their children, it is about time that Christian influence stepped in and took care of these children."[17]

"One of the Submerged" went on in the column to praise Albert Lucas's religion classes and the work of the Jewish Endeavor Society—the youth wing of the Orthodox Union that held *Shabbos* (Sabbath) services at the Educational Alliance, a Jewish-run settlement house—as examples of Jews doing their part to win the hearts and minds of their youth. But as far as the Jacob Riis House was concerned, the columnist essentially declared war. "On either side of these mission settlements there must be a Jewish settlement. We must fight them in their own way. . . . We must get rid of these missionary settlements. They have no business here."[18]

It didn't take long for Lucas himself to pile on. He made it clear from his writing that he knew who "One of the Submerged" was and numbered the person among his friends, though it's unclear whether Lucas himself had had any hand in drafting the *American Hebrew* column. A week-and-a-half later, on Orthodox Union letterhead, he wrote Riis directly, asking for clarification in a remarkably temperate letter:

Dear Sir:

I have been informed that the settlement which bears your name at 48–50 Henry Street, New York, has been conducted in a spirit not commendable to our people, so far as its religious influence is concerned. A very reliable friend of mine has also asserted that this matter has been brought to your attention, and that you have admitted that the influence of the Home is intended to be purely Christian, although the great majority of the beneficiaries of the institution are Jews.

I do not like to take hearsay evidence upon so serious a matter, for your wide influence and reputation gives the matter an importance not otherwise attachable to it.

I therefore take the liberty to request that you will favor me with a statement of your own views as to the religious influence and religious work (if any) that is carried on at the Jacob A. Riis Home, so that I may submit your answer to my executives and take such other action in this matter as may be necessary.

Yours respectfully,
Alb. Lucas, Secretary[19]

Less than a week later, Riis responded:

My Dear Sir:

There lies up on my table with your letter of inquiry one which just came from Stockbridge, Mass. It tells of the joy and sacrifice with which a number of children there have been working all summer for the little children in Henry Street, and of their delight when their fair yesterday in the rain and storm brought in $300, because of what the money would mean to so many whose homes were poor and chances few. These far-off children are the children of Christians. Their joy and their work is due to their love for a young Jew who many years ago was born into the world to show his own people and all people forever that love is the great force in all ages, the only one that has power to bridge over all differences on earth and lay hold of eternity.

In that love the work in Henry Street was begun, and in His name it has been carried on all these years. If there is anything in that "spirit not commendable to your people," I am very sorry for you. I think you are wrong. I hope you are wrong. I am glad to tell you that we have just made arrangements to buy the two houses comprised in the settlement and so make sure that the gospel of love shall be preached in that spot, at least as long as we live.

I think you will find upon inquiry that your informant is altogether wrong in assuming that the "great majority of the beneficiaries of our work" are Jews. I think he will discover that they are in quite small minority. Jews or Christians, however, they are all welcome. Their claim to our help is that they need us—their neighbors.

Faithfully yours,
Jacob A. Riis[20]

A couple of weeks later both letters were published in the *New York Post*, and in subsequent weeks the attack on Riis brought commentary from prominent uptown Jewish leaders who shared Lucas's aversion to his missionary efforts and contributed their own ideas about how to deal with the threat he and his cohorts posed. Even Catholics had issues with Riis, for the same reasons they feared Protestant influences in the public schools. But although Riis's reputation may have been somewhat tarnished, there is nothing to suggest any subsequent downturn in attendance at his mission house.[21]

Christian missions and their activities were problems that would continue to invite scrutiny from activist Jews like Lucas who distrusted them, and in subsequent years he would often speak out against them. But he also perceived a similar, and arguably more heinous, threat to which he believed the Orthodox Union needed to turn its attention: the unwelcome insinuation of the Christian religion into New York's public schools.

3

The Jews Demand That We Give Up Christmas Traditions

By mid-1903, most of Lucas's time at the Union of Orthodox Congregations was occupied with demonstrating that Christian proselytizing of the kind seen in the settlement houses was also a serious problem in the public schools. He was collecting evidence and preparing a dossier on the subject, which he first addressed at the organization's 1903 convention.[1]

Speaking in his capacity as chair of the Standing Committee on Schools and Colleges, he described the problem this way:

> We find there is a practice in many public schools in New York City to insist upon the children taking part in celebrations in honor of the Christian Savior and to indulge in ceremonials of a distinctly Christian character. We also find that hymns taken from the Christian hymnal and containing Christian doctrine are taught and sung in many schools—even in some schools where the majority, if not all, the scholars are children of our faith. We also find that there is a disinclination on the part of the children to absent themselves from the schools on days which are Jewish holidays.[2]

In his broadside, Lucas focused on celebrations and hymns; he did not specifically call out Christian influences in the textbooks, of which there were several thousand approved by the Board of Superintendents from which principals were permitted to choose. He did, however, recount the story of a young Jewish boy on the East Side who had been told to memorize a poem by Henry Wadsworth Longfellow called "The Legend of the Crossbill" that was essentially an exaltation of Jesus on the cross. When the boy refused, he was ordered by his teacher to obey. "For his disobedience," Lucas complained, "this child was punished by receiving a 'demerit for conduct.'"[3]

Lucas also reported on a meeting earlier in the year with William Henry Maxwell, New York City's superintendent of schools, the progressive son of a Presbyterian clergyman. Dr. Henry Pereira Mendes and Dr. Bernard Drachman, rabbi of the Park East Synagogue, or *Zichron Ephraim*, an anti-Reform, Orthodox congregation on the Upper East Side, had accompanied Lucas, and the men had made several points to support their case that Christianity was intruding into the schools:

- That the rule specifying that school sessions be opened with a reading of a Bible verse was generally interpreted to mean a verse from the New Testament;
- That children were being taught to sing Christian hymns that were unmistakably doctrinal and sectarian;
- That, in preparation for the winter vacation, Christmas carols and other exercises "of a distinctly Christian character" were taught and recited; and
- That children were being pressured to attend such events, even when they fell on Jewish holidays.

Lucas's crusade to make the public schools safe for Jewish students had actually begun as early as 1900, when he wrote several principals of Lower East Side schools to protest readings from the New Testament, which were offensive to Jews, as well as their efforts to compel their Jewish charges to attend school on the High Holy Days, the most sacred holidays on the Jewish calendar. Superintendent Maxwell had thus probably been made aware of these issues at least two years before the Orthodox Union lodged its formal complaint.[4]

Maxwell received the petition sympathetically. He assured Lucas and company that the board would not countenance the practices they had described and that teachers would be properly instructed so they would not recur. And he was as good as his word. On November 10, 1903, he issued Circular No. 2, 1903–4, to the district superintendents directing them to

Fig. 6. William Henry Maxwell, progressive superintendent of public schools in New York City from 1898 to 1917. Wikimedia Commons, upload .wikimedia.org/wikipedia/commons/a/a3/William_H._Maxwell.jpg.

"instruct principals that hymns containing reference to the tenets of any religious sect are out of place in unsectarian schools and should not be used."[5]

This wasn't the only religious issue with which Maxwell had to deal. He was also being pressured by local Catholics to do something about the reading of the King James Bible in the schools. In November 1903, Maxwell wrote Rev. Dr. William F. McGinnis, president of the International Catholic Truth Society, with a proposed solution. In majority Catholic schools, principals might read instead from the Catholic Douay-Rheims Bible. To facilitate this, that work would be placed on the Board of Education's official list of supplies and made available to teachers who wished to use it.[6]

REPRINTS OF LETTERS

—BY—

MR. ALBERT LUCAS

And Editorial comments from *The Hebrew Standard* in connection with the recent agitation against the proselytizing practice among the Jewish children on the East Side.

How Much Longer?

Editor, Hebrew Standard:

How much longer will the Jewish community allow itself supinely to permit its children to be led away from their Faith? How much longer will it allow the good name of our people to be smirched by those who only remember that they are Jews and owe allegiance to Israel's God, when they find themselves in positions that they themselves have brought about by their own willful heedlessness and the community's neglect?

I have been called upon this past week to investigate a case of wholestle proselytizing, that illustrates our criminal neglect and the callousness of many Jewish parents, in a way that I hope will not be allowed to continue much longer.

The New York World and some of the Yiddish papers described a breach of discipline at the Summer Home of New York Protestant Episcopal City Mission Society at Milford Haven, Conn., in the lurid head lines that nowadays are so popular. I do not enter into that part of the story, further than to say that the "disorderly" children were all Jewish girls, who had taken advantage of the offer of "God's Providence House" in Broome street to give them two weeks' vacation in the country.

Upon investigation I find: That the Sewing School in "God's Providence House" is attended very largely (if not entirely) by Jewish girls. The sessions of the Sewing School are opened by the singing of hymns, of which one is: "We are standing up for Jesus" or something to that effect. The girls were asked to give in their names if they desired to go to the country house and they were required to undergo a physical examination by the doctor and pay $1 for their fare; the two weeks' board and lodging was free. The party (74 girls, all Hebrews except 11, I am told) left on Saturday, July 1st, and after its

Fig. 7. First page of a booklet of reprinted letters by Albert Lucas concerning the proselytizing threat posed by Christian settlement houses. Courtesy American Jewish Historical Society.

The next month, Lucas published a column in which he continued his denunciation of Jacob Riis and his mission and criticized the Jewish community for being "willfully oblivious" of its duty to resist threats from missionaries like Riis. But he exonerated the Board of Education of fostering a policy of proselytizing, asserting that he believed Superintendent Maxwell was sincere in his desire to keep religion out of the classroom. The problem was not the board; it was that the board's instructions were not being carried out in the schools. He had collected many accounts of Jewish children being taught Christian hymns—sometimes by *Jewish* teachers. He even went so far as to suggest that in some cases teachers of the Jewish faith were *more* guilty than gentiles of "errors of judgment" in this area.[7]

To Lucas, Reform Jews were not much better than the gentiles determined to pull Jewish children from their religion. He actually referred to them in his convention speech as "Christless Christians of Jewish parentage." However Lucas felt about the Reform movement though, there were some issues on which most Reform leaders agreed with him, and sectarianism in the schools was one of them. In mid-1904, Rabbi Joseph Krauskopf, president of the Central Conference of American Rabbis (CCAR)—the Reform rabbinic leadership organization—plowed in right behind him on that subject. At the CCAR's fifteenth annual convention in Louisville, Kentucky, Krauskopf decried "insidious attempts" in many states to introduce readings from the New Testament and compel Jewish children to celebrate Christian holidays and sing their songs.

"Have all the Christianity you wish, cherish it as much as you can, enthrone it in your church, but keep it from our public schools," he said. He recommended that the CCAR appoint a standing committee to collect and distribute information on the evils of sectarianism.[8]

But while all Orthodox rabbis were of one mind on the issue, not all Reform rabbis were in accord. Rabbi Max Heller of Temple Sinai in New Orleans, for example, declared that limiting the public school to secular education and relegating moral and religious education to a "Sunday corner by itself" left a void that did not adequately prepare children for citizenship. He favored a regime in which a portion of the school day would be set aside for denominational instruction, an idea that would grow in acceptance over the next several years.[9]

Lucas's obsession with religious influences in the schools was not created in a vacuum. The debate had been raging all over the United States between Catholics and Protestants for most of the nineteenth century. Jews had played only a minor role in it, but that was about to change.

Fig. 8. Reform Rabbi Joseph Krauskopf, president of the Central Conference of American Rabbis, who shared Albert Lucas's concern over proselytizing in the public schools. Wikimedia Commons, upload .wikimedia.org/wikipedia/commons/3/39/Joseph_Krauskopf.jpg.

In September 1901, the Cleveland, Ohio, school council had passed a resolution intended to improve "the morals as well as the mental capacities" of its children by mandating the teaching of the Lord's Prayer, the Ten Commandments, and the twenty-third psalm in the public schools. Local Reform Rabbi Moses Gries of Temple Tifereth Israel immediately criticized the move, asserting that "religious teaching by its very nature is sectarian" and had no place in a public school. The council, which apparently never anticipated the degree of opposition its action would engender, was heavily lobbied by Jews and Catholics to reverse itself, and it quickly did so.[10]

That same year, the parents of a Los Angeles boy complained that their son had been required to chant the Christmas carol "Away in a Manger" at school. This prompted Hungarian-born rabbi Sigmund Hecht, the spiritual leader of local Reform Congregation B'nai B'rith, to examine the song books approved by the local board of education. He found many hymns that made direct reference to the divinity of Christ, something he insisted violated the laws of the state of California. His effort got mixed reviews. The Los Angeles *Express* insisted he and his Jewish brethren should "bow to the will of the majority," while Salt Lake City's *Deseret Evening News*, the official organ of the Church of the Latter-day Saints (Mormon), asserted that "in this country, the minority has a right to protest against teaching the religion of the majority in any public school."[11]

The subject came up in St. Joseph, Missouri, in 1903 when local Jews complained about a principal who insisted the Lord's Prayer be recited each day. She was not ordered to cease, but rather counseled by the assistant superintendent of schools to be more careful. "So long as no one objects it is all right; otherwise, it is not," the *Jewish Voice* quoted him as saying. That same year, California took an entirely different tack. In April 1903, citing the state constitution, its attorney general declared that public school teachers were *not* permitted to read from the Scriptures. "It is impossible to find any version of the Bible which does not represent and promulgate the teaching of some religious sect or society," he wrote.[12]

Then, in 1905, the issue arose in both Philadelphia and New Haven. A Jewish teacher who headed up a Philadelphia kindergarten was criticized in the *Christian Statesman* for suppressing the customary Christmas and Easter exercises. This incident was raised in the context of a xenophobic rant about the crisis caused by the recent influx of non-Christian immigrants. The paper exhorted Christians to "stand together in the defense of the Christian elements in our national life," lest they be "swept away."[13]

In New Haven, after the parents of two Jewish children objected to the singing of Christmas carols, Jacob Ullman, a Jewish judge at the county's Court of Common Pleas and a member of the board of education, prevailed on the local superintendent of schools to ban them from the closing exercises that preceded the winter vacation. The superintendent complied and immediately came in for a raft of criticism. "We had to give up the saying of the Lord's Prayer to satisfy the Catholics, and now the Jews demand that we give up Christmas traditions," a local Protestant businessman complained. But not all Jews supported the demand; some local Jewish parents preferred not to make an issue of it.[14]

Back in New York, however, Albert Lucas had no hesitation in making an issue of it. And Principal Frank Harding in Brooklyn had provided him with just the opening he needed to do it.

4
An Unfit Man

After P.S. 144 closed on Tuesday, December 19, 1905, the day of Principal Harding's assembly speech, Gussie Herbert began the five-minute walk up Howard Avenue to her family's flat at 2093 Dean Street. She did not get far, however, before some Christian boys in the neighborhood began to torment her. They called her a "Christ killer" and a "sheeny," a popular, but thoroughly offensive, slang term for a Jew. Someone also spat in her face. She said later that she had approached a policeman for protection but had been rebuffed.

"Why don't you walk on the other side?" he had said to her before turning on his heel and walking away.[1]

At dinner that evening, she told her father what had transpired at school: that her principal had exhorted all of the students to be more like Jesus; that she had challenged him about making such remarks in a public school setting; that he had remonstrated with her and ordered her to sit down or leave the room; and that for her efforts, she had subsequently been harassed by gentile children.

The story enraged, but did not surprise, thirty-eight-year-old Edward Herbert, a prominent attorney with an office at 63 Park Row, the tony headquarters of Joseph Pulitzer's *New York World* and one of the most prestigious addresses in the city. Herbert, something of an activist in local Jewish affairs, had emigrated to the United States from his native Romania in 1882 and a few years later married Sophia Schwartz, also Romanian-born and three years his junior. The couple had lived in Lower Manhattan when they became

Fig. 9. Edward Herbert, Augusta Herbert's father, a prominent attorney and activist in local Jewish affairs. *Hebrew Standard,* July 9, 1915. National Library of Israel.

naturalized citizens in 1893, and by 1905 had relocated to Brooklyn, where he was already well connected in the local Jewish community. At fourteen, Gussie was the eldest of their four children.

Nor was Gussie the only child who went home with such a story that night. Many Jewish students gave their parents similar accounts of the assembly, and it did not take long for Jewish Brownsville to be up in arms. Apart from Herbert, several prominent figures in the community were also agitated. In hastily called meetings, local business and fraternal organizations, including a couple of Masonic lodges, took up the matter. There was even some talk of organizing a mass meeting, though one never materialized.[2]

None of the parents bothered to circle back to the principal to ask his version of the event, in part because Herbert subsequently interviewed some twenty of Gussie's schoolmates, all of whom corroborated her account. Then, too, the story was very believable because it was not Harding's first such transgression in the eyes of the community, and he had been warned against another one. Some ten days earlier, it had been Herbert himself who had written the principal to caution against the holding of semireligious services in the school and the decoration of the school walls with icons "offensive to the Jewish faith." Harding had acknowledged Herbert's letter and promised to give it his immediate attention.[3]

It thus may have been no coincidence that it was Herbert's daughter who rose to challenge Harding. The civic-minded Edward Herbert had an abiding interest in the affairs of immigrant Jews like himself and his family. He had once taken out an advertisement in the Yiddish-language *Forverts* offering free legal services to Jewish laborers suing their employers to get paid. The subject of religion in the schools had almost certainly come up at the family dinner table in the past.

Unwilling to let the matter go, Herbert decided to bring it to Albert Lucas. The men had known each other since 1898 and Gussie had been a student in Lucas's religion class at the First Roumanian-American Synagogue on Rivington Street before the Herbert family relocated to Brooklyn. Aware of Lucas's ongoing investigation of Christianizing influences in the schools, Herbert assumed he would be interested in what had gone on at P.S. 144. He asserted in his letter to Lucas that "this deplorable condition prevails also in other schools in Brownsville," adding, "I must most urgently and emphatically ask you to use your utmost endeavors to abate this nuisance."[4]

Within two days, a petition was circulating in Brownsville. It included Herbert's letters to Harding and Lucas as attachments, and quickly amassed some one hundred signatures. It read, in part:

> To the Honorable School Board of Education, District Number 39, New York City:
>
> The undersigned taxpayers and residents of the city of New York do respectfully complain and bring to the notice of this honorable board the following:
>
> That F. F. Harding, principal of the School No. 144, has established a policy to systematically Christianize children born and raised in the

Fig. 10. P.S. 144, an elementary school in Brooklyn's Brownsville neighborhood with an overwhelmingly Jewish student body, as it appeared in 1904. Brooklyn Public Library.

> Jewish faith, and for that purpose has at various times and particularly at the time hereinafter mentioned conducted quasi-religious services in the assembly room of said school at which time he took occasion to read passages from the New Testament and sing sectarian hymns, knowing that such tactics are in disaccord with the Jewish religion, and detrimental to the education of children of Jewish parentage. That he has permitted and has tolerated the classrooms in said school to be decorated with images of saints and of the Madonna, a practice which is contrary to the American spirit, and in violation of the rules of the Board of Education.[5]

The District 39 School Committee was the right place to go to demand an investigation into Harding's conduct. It was one of fourteen local school committees in Brooklyn alone (there were forty-six in all of New York City). All bore responsibility for visiting and inspecting the schools in their respective districts, taking note of the state of the facilities and monitoring the attendance of teachers and pupils and the observance of the law and of board regulations. They were empowered, among other things, to investigate charges leveled against faculty and staff and to recommend fines or dismissals where appropriate, but their decisions were not final. All were subject to review by the New York City Board of Education.[6]

Harding's accusers maintained that as an immediate consequence of his sermon, several Jewish children—not just Gussie Herbert—had been victimized by Christian classmates. Consequently, the petition went on, "the tendency of said principal is to create hatred and prejudice between the children as against one another, and to create strife among them, and cause Jewish children to be persecuted by their fellow classmates." Finally, it demanded his dismissal, calling him unfit to be in charge of a public school.[7]

Gussie was interviewed by several newspapers and her story remained consistent. When a reporter from the *Brooklyn Standard Union* showed Harding the comments she had attributed to him, however, he categorically denied having made them. "The only statement . . . that is true is 'have more pleasure in giving than in receiving,'" Harding insisted. "The statement as a whole is so garbled and falsified that I characterize it as utterly untruthful. I never made any such statements, nor sought in any manner to influence any child in religious matters."[8]

Albert Lucas had anticipated that something like the Harding affair might happen during the Christmas season. A few days before Christmas, the *Brooklyn Daily Eagle* had laid out school celebration plans for the borough, and they were anything but mindful of Jewish sensibilities. The paper went out of its way to gush about how inclusive and meaningful the programs would be to all, insisting that the festivities—which, at P.S. 108, for example, were to include singing of "O Holy Night"—would be "enjoyed by Jew and Gentile, Ethiopian and Caucasian, rich and poor, kindergarten and high school."[9]

The *Eagle* was giving voice to a sincere belief on the part of many Christians for whom the holiday felt less like a religious celebration than a seasonal, cultural—even patriotic—festival. What that view did not take into account was how a people like immigrant Jews, subject in their countries of origin to discrimination and sometimes even to forced conversions, might perceive it as an existential threat.

That is certainly how Albert Lucas saw it. Each holiday season, he reminded Jewish children in his classes to be alert for "bribes" in the form of Christmas toys and treats. This year, just a few days before the P.S. 144 assembly, he had issued a warning to their parents in a letter published in both the *Hebrew Standard* and the *American Hebrew and Jewish Messenger*. He reminded all that Superintendent Maxwell had made it clear two years earlier that sectarian hymns were prohibited in the schools.[10]

"I call upon Jewish parents to inquire into the details of what their children are being asked to do in their schools during the next couple of weeks," he wrote, and to see to it that their children "do not take part in any celebration that partakes in any way of being a Christmas festival."[11]

And that is just what the concerned Brownsville parents attempted to do with their petition, albeit after the fact. Lucas himself did not immediately weigh in on Harding's performance, but lest anyone think it an isolated case, he wrote in the *American Hebrew* about a shocking article that had appeared that month in *Frank Leslie's Weekly*, a popular, large-format, illustrated literary and news publication with tens of thousands of subscribers nationwide. It was nothing less than a step-by-step "how to" guide to indoctrinating non-Christian children with the "symbols and joys" of Christmas.

Written by a Charles C. Johnson, the article asserted that the joy and gift-giving of the Christmas season was the best way to "improve" the homes of immigrants. It took the reader from familiarizing children with simple toys to sending them out for an evergreen tree, bringing it into the classroom and trimming it, placing presents beneath it, and finally distributing the gifts. And it was illustrated with a full page of photographs of East Side children over the caption "Benighted Children Taught to Celebrate Christmas." Although the youngsters were not explicitly identified as Jews, it was abundantly clear which "benighted" children the author was talking about. Immigrant Christian children needed no introduction to Christmas.[12]

Lucas took the article as prima facie evidence of a conspiracy within the public schools to "break down the religious observance of the Jewish children of the East Side." To his mind, it was a plot even more nefarious than the "snares and baits" of the settlement houses. He made no room for the possibility that some deeply religious Christians like Frank Harding might simply be touting the superiority of their faith without necessarily explicitly intending a mission to gain converts to it.

What was actually going on in the New York schools, however, despite the alarming, step-by-step Christianization guide detailed in *Leslie's Weekly*, was a good deal more benign than the bald-faced conversion efforts of the Christian settlement houses that kept count of the number of souls they brought to Jesus. Those in charge of the school system, progressives like Superintendent Maxwell, were not interested in saving souls, but they did believe that the schools' responsibility to promote the acculturation and Americanization of immigrant students meant playing a paternalistic role in areas like civic and values education. Because many principals and teachers conflated being good Americans with being good Christians, they naturally gravitated to Christian symbols, traditions, and lore when attempting to inculcate moral values in their charges. It's likely Frank Harding fell into this category. Although there was certainly a subtext in his remarks that undermined Judaism, when he told the *Standard Union* that he had never had any intention of proselytizing, he was probably telling the truth.[13]

There was also evidence—ignored by Lucas—that some schools were actually going out of their way to accommodate the beliefs of their Jewish students. For example, some fifty-five hundred girls in thirty of Manhattan's public schools were being instructed in cooking. In addition to the arts of roasting, frying, baking, and canning, they were learning how to measure and shop for food and how to care for the home. But at P.S. 147, whose student population was composed entirely of the children of Orthodox Jewish families, for example, the girls were permitted to buy the meat from kosher butchers, and the tableware and cookware were separated into one set for meat dishes and another for dairy dishes.[14]

As 1905 came to a close, there was no word from the District 39 School Committee as to when it intended to launch an investigation into Principal Harding's alleged "systematic Christianization" of his school's students. Many believed the delay was a deliberate effort to buy time in order to make the

December 7, 1905 LESLIE'S WEEKLY 545

EXPLAINING CHRISTMAS TO KINDERGARTEN CHILDREN WHO ARE IGNORANT OF ITS MEANING.

TEACHING THE YOUNGSTERS THE USE OF TOYS.

PUPILS STARTING OUT TO GET THE CHRISTMAS-TREE.

PROCESSION BRINGING THE TREE INTO THE SCHOOL-ROOM.

THE TREE WITH ITS LOAD OF GIFTS AN OBJECT OF ADMIRATION.

DELIGHTED CHILDREN ENJOYING THE NEW AND NOVEL TOYS ALLOTTED TO THEM.

BENIGHTED CHILDREN TAUGHT TO CELEBRATE CHRISTMAS.

LITTLE PUPILS IN NEW YORK'S PUBLIC SCHOOLS, WHO HAVE NOT KNOWN WHAT THE GREAT FESTIVAL MEANS, INDUCTED INTO ITS SYMBOLS AND JOYS.—*Photographs by C. C. Johnson.* *See opposite page.*

Fig. 11. Illustrations accompanying an article in *Frank Leslie's Weekly* praising efforts to initiate "benighted"—read, Jewish—immigrant children into the "symbols and joys" of Christmas through the public schools. *Frank Leslie's Weekly*, December 7, 1905.

whole matter go away as memories faded. But several made it clear to the *Brooklyn Citizen* that such a strategy would not succeed.[15]

The *Hebrew Standard,* which had often given space to Albert Lucas's missives on Christian influences in the schools, insisted that Harding's proselytizing efforts were worse than any it had seen in the past. Noting that Augusta Herbert's schoolmates had given her the nickname of "Deborah," a reference to the biblical prophetess and warrior who had called for an attack on the Canaanites, it warned that the Jewish community would have "only itself to blame if it supinely allows itself to suffer at the hands of officials who mistake the scope of their authority."[16]

5
Systematically Christianizing

During the second week of January 1906, the signatories to the petition to remove Principal Harding received letters from the District 39 School Committee. The body planned to hold a hearing on the case at P.S. 84 on Glenmore Avenue on the afternoon of Saturday, January 13.

How the committee members could have thought that inviting Jewish parents, many, if not most of whom were Orthodox, to a business meeting on their Sabbath was a good idea is puzzling, since the committee chairman, Baruch Miller, was himself a Jew. The thirty-year-old, Austrian-born Miller, a father of two, had immigrated in 1885 and was a naturalized citizen. Fluent in Yiddish and active in the political and civil life of Brownsville, he was a real estate attorney and served as the chief interpreter in the King's County court system. He also sat on the board of the Hebrew Educational Society of Brooklyn, a local, Jewish-run settlement house.[1]

Miller was probably not as religiously observant as many of his neighbors, however, because the date of the meeting had actually been his idea. According to the *Brooklyn Daily Eagle*, he had deliberately chosen a Saturday, thinking that there wasn't much difference between going to the theater, which many local Jews *did* do on their Sabbath, and coming to a hearing. It is also possible, of course, that he had chosen the date as a means of suppressing attendance at what was sure to be a contentious meeting. In any event, he soon received a pointed phone call from Albert Lucas, who insisted on an alternate date because attending a Saturday meeting at which business was conducted was absolutely forbidden for religious Jews. The hearing was thus postponed until the evening of the following Wednesday, January 17.[2]

Everyone wondered what Harding's defense would be, because after his initial statement to the *Brooklyn Standard Union* that Augusta Herbert's account was wrong in nearly all aspects, he had kept silent. A friend, however, defended him to the *New York Sun*. "Mr. Harding has always been careful not to say anything or do anything to offend the Jews," the person told the *Sun* reporter. "He has had many Jewish pupils and he knows how they feel on the subject of religion. He has always felt Jews were his friends, and when the charges were first brought against him, some of us who know him well would not believe that such action could have been taken. It seemed to us that Mr. Herbert must have had some personal grudge against the principal."[3]

There was no evidence that Herbert's problem with Harding was personal, and in fact there was some indication that Harding had actually been popular with Jews in the past. Among the students at P.S. 144 were the inmates of the Brooklyn Hebrew Orphan Asylum on Ralph Avenue, who, ironically, were there only *because* of him. They had attended nearby P.S. 83 when he had presided over that school, and when the officers of the asylum learned of his impending transfer to P.S. 144, they had asked that the orphans be permitted to transfer there as well.[4]

Dr. Milton Reizenstein, superintendent of the Hebrew Educational Society, a body established in Brownsville in 1899 by Abraham Abraham (the Jewish retailer of Abraham and Straus fame) to improve the physical and intellectual condition of poor Jews, explained to a *Brooklyn Daily Eagle* reporter that despite the language of the petition, the proceedings were not directed at Harding personally; it was the practice of using the platform of a public school to promote a religious holiday that was at issue. That, he said, was why the Union of Orthodox Jewish Congregations had been tapped to serve as counsel for the complainants.

Herbert himself, who had three children at P.S. 144 and had instigated the whole affair, did not actually sign the petition to remove Harding, nor did he attend the hearing. He left it to Isidore Hirschfield, a New York–born attorney of German-Jewish extraction, and his colleague, Albert Lucas, who were both secretaries of the Orthodox Union, to present the charges.[5]

The hearing—the first of its kind in which a principal had been accused of proselytizing—took the form of a trial, with witnesses for and against Harding invited to testify. Long before the stated start time of eight p.m., a huge crowd had gathered outside P.S. 84. When people were finally allowed into the building, the *Brooklyn Citizen* reported, "they swept up the narrow stairs like a great wave, filling the auditorium with tossing, heaving forms and waving arms, and overflowing into the adjoining classrooms."

Some fifteen hundred people quickly packed the assembly hall in the school's boys' wing, among them P.S. 144 parents and their friends as well as principals of other schools and many teachers. Harding had seen to it that his supporters were well represented. The four policemen sent to keep order were unequal to the task of stopping people from crowding the aisles and doors—violating the fire laws—and were forced to telephone for reinforcements. They also tried to limit the children entering the schoolhouse to those who were slated to testify.[6]

How Jewish the audience was depended on which newspaper you read. Although the *American Hebrew and Jewish Messenger* found it remarkable how few Jews were in attendance, the *Brooklyn Citizen*, which was supportive of the principal and unsympathetic to the complainants, claimed the audience was predominantly Jewish and added that it included a sizeable number who believed the proceedings absurd. "Harding's career," it wrote, "had been placed in jeopardy by what many considered merely an insignificant bit of poor taste, turned from the molehill into the mountain by an excitable little girl backed up by an equally excitable father and his three score impetuous friends and coreligionists." The reporter admitted that only a few Jewish members of the audience had actually expressed opposition to the proceedings, but even the Yiddish-language *Die Wahrheit* confirmed the presence of two distinct Jewish factions: one that considered Harding a proselytizer who sought any opportunity to promote Christianity and the other that denied he had advocated anything of the kind.[7]

When Harding appeared, it was, by all accounts, to tumultuous cheers, and when Augusta Herbert and her classmates entered the room they were hissed. But there is no evidence to suggest that either reaction was coming specifically from the Jews in attendance. The *Hebrew Standard* made it a point to reprove most of the female teachers present for their obvious animosity toward the girl. Once all the witnesses had assembled, the members of the school board entered. All had been appointed by the president of the Borough of Brooklyn. Apart from Miller, the chair, there were six others, one of whom, former congressman Mitchell May, a member of the city board of education who had been assigned to district 39, was also Jewish.[8]

Miller's first act was to order the removal of the children who were to be witnesses in the case, lest they be swayed by others' testimony. This elicited objections from the audience, and Harding himself asked that they be permitted to stay but was overruled. When the children were slow to leave, Miller threatened to hold the proceedings in executive session. After they had finally departed, their seats were filled immediately by adults who had been standing in the hall.

Harding asked that Gussie Herbert, who did not seem at all shaken by the reception she had received from the crowd, be excused with the others, but here again, Miller overruled him. "The chair decides that the witness will remain," he announced. "She is the complainant as well as a witness."

At Harding's request, the charges against him were read in full and he was asked how he wished to plead. Before he would respond, he demanded to know the section of the New York City Charter under which he was being tried so he might understand how to appeal the case to a higher authority if need be. After consulting with the other board members and Attorney Hirschfield, Miller announced that the charges were being brought under Section 1098, which set out the duties of local committees like his, instructing them to visit all the schools in their respective districts at least once a quarter to inspect local schools and to determine, among other things, "whether or not the provisions of the school laws in respect to the teaching of sectarian doctrines or the use of sectarian books have been violated." Hearing this, Harding offered a plea of not guilty.[9]

The first thing Hirschfield did in his opening statement was to drop the charge of "systematically Christianizing," surely the most difficult of all the allegations to prove, and very likely not true of Harding anyway. He said

Fig. 12. Dr. Frank Fountain Harding, Presbyterian principal of Brownsville's P.S. 144, who exhorted the students in his school to be "more like Jesus." Courtesy Frank F. Harding.

frankly that he thought Harding had better judgment than to have attempted that. Harding was also not to be blamed, he asserted, for any assaults against Jewish children by their schoolmates off the school grounds. Ironically, Harding *himself* objected to the withdrawal of the "systematically Christianizing" charge, however. He insisted the allegation be thoroughly explored because it had tarnished his reputation and his honor. After all, the petitioners had labeled him unfit for his job and had demanded his removal. It is also likely that he wished the charge to stand because he believed it could easily be disproved.

But it was ultimately up to his accusers, and not to him, to specify the allegations against him, and Hirschfield had wisely left only four of them in place. It was no accident that all were matters of fact rather than interpretation:

- That Harding had read extracts from the New Testament at the school;
- That there had been singing of sectarian songs and hymns and recitation of the Lord's Prayer;
- That sectarian pictures and images had been displayed in the school's classrooms;
- That Harding had commented on the Scriptures.

Most importantly, Hirschfield did not repeat the demand in the petition that Harding be discharged from his position.[10]

Gussie Herbert was the first witness called, and she acquitted herself well. She was poised as she answered the questions put to her. Her story did not vary from what she had said earlier, but she added that every Tuesday at assembly, Principal Harding gave a Bible reading from a book with a red cover. That book was produced and she identified it; it was not the Bible itself, but rather William J. Shearer's *Gems of Wisdom from Bible Literature and Proverbs.*

She could not recall the specific hymns she and her schoolmates had been asked to sing on the day of the principal's sermon, but reported that she had seen a picture of the Madonna and child, cut from a newspaper, on the wall of her sister's classroom. And finally, she allowed that when Harding recited the Lord's Prayer, he had not required the students to say it along with him. They had merely been told to bow their heads.

Harding, who was not represented by counsel, questioned Gussie himself. He got her to admit that she was unsure whether the Bible verses he had quoted were from the Old or New Testament and reminded her that although songs had been sung about holly and Santa Claus, there had been no reference to Christ in any of them. But he was unable to shake her from her basic narrative, which had, in all essentials, been the same since she first recounted it on December 19.

Hirschfield called Harding to the stand next; it is unclear whether the Constitution's Fifth Amendment right to decline to testify against oneself

Fig. 13. Cover of *Gems of Wisdom from Bible Literature and Proverbs,* a collection of quotations from Scripture (New York: Richardson, Smith, 1904). Library of Congress.

applied to a school board hearing as it did to a court of law, but in any event Harding, eager to clear his name, did not object to being questioned.

"Do you ever read the Lord's Prayer?" Hirschfield asked the principal.

"I don't have to read it. I *know* it," Harding replied.

"Were there strings of holly in the classrooms?"

"I didn't take particular notice."

"Were there bunches of holly?" Hirschfield pressed.

"I'm not very much up on those things. Yes, I suppose so."

When Harding objected to the line of questioning, Hirschfield explained himself. "I offer this because we claim that Christmas trees and holly and such things are a part of sectarian teaching, and that under the laws of the state, and according to Superintendent Maxwell's orders, any celebration of Christmas in the public schools is absolutely forbidden. I am bringing to the attention of the board the fact that Christmas exercises *were* held, so that it can take action on its own volition."

Harding allowed that he *had* made reference to Christmas, but, he insisted, not to Christ. He acknowledged having received Edward Herbert's letter and insisted he had been mindful of the warning in it not to hold religious services in the classrooms or to decorate the premises with icons Jews might find offensive.

"On December 11, at a teachers' meeting, I said that as Christmas time was approaching, I desired them to be careful, and not to have any songs or recitations that would be likely to offend any child. I said that I did not think any reference to Christ as divine or as the Savior would be proper. I cautioned them, I said, as I had received a letter on the subject, and did not desire any conflict with religious feeling in the classrooms."

But then he added that he had not forbidden the holding of Christmas exercises.

He claimed to have ordered the removal of images of the Madonna and Christ in the Temple from some classrooms. Asked point blank whether he had used the words "Christ blesses everyone but hypocrites, and hypocrites are those who do not believe in him" during the December 19 assembly, he flatly denied ever having made the remark, which was the crux of the case against him. Sympathetic members of the audience applauded.[11]

At that point, after only two witnesses had been heard, Chairman Miller adjourned the hearing, which had already gone on for nearly four hours, over Harding's objections.

The *Brooklyn Citizen* found the entire session a farce. It had been quite disorderly, because Miller had been unequal to the task of running it. To the paper, he seemed nervous, hostile to Harding, and unable to control the audience. At one point, when a man interrupted the proceedings, Miller had ordered him removed, only to be rebuffed by the police, who claimed they had no authority to eject him unless Miller wished to press charges against him.[12]

The *Brooklyn Daily Eagle* asserted that many Brownsville Jews were unsympathetic to the attack on Principal Harding. It wrote, "Intelligent Hebrews in Brownsville . . . regret the publicity given to the case, and have said that while Mr. Harding did not probably exercise good judgment, an intimation to him through the district superintendent or a member of the Board of Education that he was violating the law would have been all that was necessary."

That, of course, was essentially what Edward Herbert had tried to do several days before Christmas; he had warned Harding and had been ignored. The *Eagle* made no mention of that. The paper did, however, print the text of a second petition then in circulation in the borough that had already garnered some sixteen hundred signatures:

> We, the citizens of this Christian land of liberty, the haven of the oppressed, the home of the most liberal contributors of funds to alleviate oppression wherever it may be than any other country, emphatically, indignantly and earnestly protest against any action being taken condemnatory of principal Frank F. Harding, of Public School number 144, Howard Avenue, Brooklyn, for his patriotic advice given to the children of his school, but rather commend him for his utterances, as they are in keeping with the doctrines and teachings of the moral and political laws which have caused the United States of America to be the asylum of the oppressed of all the earth.[13]

The *Eagle* did not go so far as to assert that Jewish names had been among the signatories, however, and it is doubtful many were. It is not difficult to believe that there were Jews in Brooklyn embarrassed by the brouhaha Herbert, Lucas, and the Orthodox Union were making over Principal Harding's remarks. Jewish activism of any kind often upset the more established Jews who jealously guarded their own fragile acceptance by gentile New Yorkers. That had happened, for example, when Lower East Side Jews had organized a boycott of kosher butchers in 1902 as a means to lower the price of meat that had degenerated into violence on the streets.[14]

But it strains credulity that any Jews—established *or* newly arrived—would have *commended* Harding for his words and actions, much less accepted the portrayal of America as a "Christian land of liberty." It is far more likely that those behind the petition were Harding's gentile allies, many of whom, probably not unlike Harding himself, believed that public schools should be agents of moral instruction, and were oblivious to how threatened some Jews felt when this appeared in Christian clothing.

Die Wahrheit, a Yiddish-language, socialist paper that competed with the *Forverts*, was sure whoever was behind the petition had a far more nefarious agenda than simply protecting Harding. The paper detected a vast antisemitic conspiracy in Brooklyn. Without naming names, it insisted that "the Christians around Brownsville had already shown several times that they see Jews as enemies." Some, it speculated, were simply angry about the many changes to their community that had come with the arrival of multitudes of Jews, rising rents chief among them. And others, it added, "simply don't like Jews." Among the latter were Germans "who long strongly for the antisemitic movement of the fatherland." They, the paper believed, were the impetus behind the petition.[15]

The backlash continued. *Die Wahrheit* reported on a teacher at Brooklyn's Erasmus Hall High School who, presumably inspired by Harding's example, defiantly preached Christianity to his Jewish pupils. And that same week, the Rev. William Sheafe Chase, rector of the Episcopalian Christ Church on Brooklyn's Bedford Avenue, delivered a patronizing sermon deeply critical of the Jewish community's stance against Harding.[16]

"There are some people in this country who do not clearly understand the nature of the religious freedom which has given to the Jews and other non-Christian peoples a greater toleration and a larger sympathy for them and their faiths than now exists in any other country of the world," he opined.

"Every American citizen should realize that while the United States is a nation without an established church, it is not, and should not be, a nation without a religion," he went on to insist. To back up this thesis, he asserted that Christianity was a part of the common law of the land; that it had always been the custom in America to observe Sunday, "the Christian day of the resurrection," as a holiday; and that because public schools are supported by public money in their mission, it followed, as far as he was concerned, that "whatever is necessary to produce the best moral training must have its place in the schools."

He concluded that "there must, then, be some religion in our public schools." And he had no doubt about which religion it should be.[17]

6

I Will Speak about Christ as Much as I Want To

Attendance was strictly controlled when the proceedings at P.S. 84 resumed on January 30. This time, passes had been issued to those who had business before the school committee and no one else was admitted by the Brownsville police, who had been dispatched in force to patrol the streets outside the building and guard the doors. The *Eagle* judged that the audience, about six hundred people for this second round, was about evenly divided between those who did, and did not, sympathize with Principal Harding.

By now, Harding had retained counsel. Attorneys James G. Wallace, Jr., and Morris W. Hart—the latter a Jew—appeared and offered their first motion when the hearing began at 8:20 p.m. It was to throw out all testimony from the previous session, when Harding had represented himself, on the grounds that the proceedings had been irregular and the shorthand transcript of the session was garbled. Their motion, which asked that the case be heard again from the beginning, was denied. They also insisted on putting Gussie Herbert back on the stand so they might cross-examine her, but Hirschfield objected and she was not recalled.

After discussion, however, Chairman Miller did rule that only testimony that related directly to what had occurred in the P.S. 144 assembly on December 19 would be admitted. That meant that the charges concerning the display of sectarian images in the classrooms and the singing of Christian songs at other times had essentially been dismissed.

Hirschfield called only a few more witnesses before resting his case. All were girls who had been present in the assembly hall. Fifteen-year-olds Polly Myerson and Rose Levine remembered Harding's remark about Christ and hypocrites just as Gussie Herbert had stated it. Kate Schlessel, also fifteen, recollected Harding telling the boys and girls to be like Christ. And fourteen-year-old Alice Weinzimmer recalled both statements, and on cross-examination recounted that she had considered them offensive to Jewish children.

Harding's attorneys had decided to fight fire with fire, and they began by calling students of their own choosing. Fourteen-year-old Celia Cohen, their first witness, remembered Harding saying, "We should show the Christmas spirit of peace and good will toward men," and that "it is better to give than to receive." After Gussie Herbert had asked her question, Celia recalled, the principal had said, "I will speak about Christ as much as I want to, as I would speak of any other historical character." She also remembered him telling Gussie that if she did not like what he had to say, she—or anybody else—could leave the room.

Samuel Rothman, thirteen, a boy from the Hebrew Orphan Asylum, remembered the principal telling students it was a time to be cheerful and to help the poor. He also recalled a remark about hypocrites, but not a mention of Jesus. He hadn't heard Gussie's question, but he did remember Harding telling her to take her seat. On cross-examination, Samuel admitted to having been called to Harding's office twice and asked to repeat what he had heard, but he insisted that neither Harding nor any of his teachers had instructed him on what to say.

After more of the same with two more student witnesses, some teachers were called. Anna C. Hawley, who taught the graduating class, did recall Harding mentioning that Christ had brought a message of peace and good will, and his defending his right to speak of Christ after Gussie's question, just as Celia Cohen had. Another teacher, Bertha B. Knoche, said essentially the same thing. A third teacher, who gave evidence for Harding, was described by the *Hebrew Standard* as Jewish.[1]

Paul Lazarus, superintendent of the Brooklyn Hebrew Orphan Asylum, stated he would not have sent the 250 young residents of the asylum to P.S. 144 had he thought Mr. Harding held the attitudes reflected in the charges against him. But Hirschfield protested and his objection was sustained.

Then Harding's attorneys recalled the principal himself, this time to ask him precisely what he *had* said on December 19. He did not deny having mentioned Jesus Christ, as he had during the earlier hearing. He said he had told the pupils about conditions in the Roman Empire when Christ came, that his message had been one of peace and good will, and that he had spoken harshly of hypocrites. He categorically denied ever having said, "boys and girls, be like Christ," "Christ likes all but the hypocrites," "Have feelings of Christ in you," or "Christ is Lord."

Asked about his reprimand of Gussie Herbert, he described her as having been rude, insulting, and insubordinate and said, "I was somewhat astonished at her coming to me and speaking like that, and I told her to take her seat." He had then asserted his right to speak of Jesus just as he might any other historical figure.[2]

Harding survived cross-examination. His attorneys stepped in when Chairman Miller asked him if ever, during his career, he had had any complaints preferred against him. They instructed him not to answer.

"Do you refuse to answer because it would tend to degrade and incriminate you?" Miller persisted.

"He refuses by advice of his counsel," attorney Wallace responded.

"Is it not a fact that you have been charged with teaching sectarian doctrines?" Hirschfield asked. But opposing counsel objected again and the objection was sustained.

The session ended just after midnight without action by the committee. The chairman announced that a decision would be forthcoming, but before he adjourned the meeting, he gave the attorneys two weeks to present briefs, not on questions of fact, but on the law.

The *Brooklyn Citizen*, which had deemed the committee's earlier session farcical, thought this one a decided improvement. Not only were both sides represented by counsel, but the audience was better behaved and Miller seemed better prepared. But the paper still graded him harshly for his

Fig. 14. A street in Brownsville, Brooklyn, New York, as it appeared in 1907. MOA Art / Old NYC Photos. Author's collection.

running of the meeting, noting that he frequently had to resort to banging his gavel to keep order.[3]

As some Jews had feared, the case generated a good deal of ill-feeling in the gentile community, and much sympathy for Principal Harding. A letter writer to the *Eagle* who signed his missive "Truly American"—the obvious implication being that the Jews who were complaining were something else—decried the "rather burlesque performance, in which an honored principal of our public schools was held up to ridicule by a number of children of his school." He complained that Gussie Herbert had been made a heroine "for demoralizing a public school and attacking the methods of America's most sacred institution," adding that "her example of defiance is a menace to our educational system." He ended his letter ominously: "We know where danger lurks and how to fortify the schools that will ever be truly American."[4]

Surely not coincidentally, two days after the hearing someone played a prank on Miller. He woke up at his home to discover that in the wee hours of the morning, someone had maliciously planted a Christmas tree on his front lawn.[5]

Not surprisingly, the Principals' Association of the City of New York sprang to the defense of one of their own, unanimously adopting a resolution extending their sympathy to him and expressing confidence in his abilities. This prompted "Truly American" to put pen to paper again to suggest that the principals go even further and prosecute "all guilty of deliberate misstatements." He spewed venom this time not only at the Herbert girl, but also at Baruch Miller, who, he claimed, "injudiciously and in the presence of hundreds of teachers and school children, stated that it was 'a case of veracity between the principal and a pupil', while his attitude was decidedly in favor of the pupil."[6]

The Jewish papers, of course, saw things entirely differently. The *Tageblatt* thought Isidore Hirschfield and Albert Lucas had performed brilliantly and proven their case and that the children had been inspired witnesses who had shown persuasively that the schools were teaching them "things they should not be learning."[7]

Before the two-week deadline for briefs had passed, the school committee received a letter from Hirschfield asking for an extension; he and Lucas wanted to examine how other states treated the issue of Christmas in the schools. He was granted ten more days. Their brief was finally submitted in early March. Among the points they raised were:

- Harding had violated the prohibitions against the teaching of religion and the making of any note or comment on the Holy Scriptures;
- Harding's use of the book *Gems of Wisdom* was unauthorized and a violation of the bylaws of the Board of Education;
- The use of Christmas trees was prohibited in the public schools, and purely Christian pictures and icons had no place on the walls of school rooms;
- The recital of any prayer is prohibited by law.

As far as the plaintiffs were concerned, they had wisely concluded that the overall issue of religion in the public schools was far more important than punishing Frank Harding, even though his own testimony, to their minds, had established his guilt. The complainants did not seek his dismissal; contrary to the original petition, the brief was clear that "a scalp is not prayed for."

But they believed that an example still needed to be made of him, so they asked only for his transfer.[8]

Because the bad press the Jews were getting over the Harding case had alarmed some of his fellow Jews and made them unsure of the wisdom of pressing it, Albert Lucas felt it necessary to publish a letter in the *American Hebrew and Jewish Messenger* before the school committee was to rule on the case. He wanted to address the criticism that the effort was liable to lead to dangerous consequences for Jews in America.

He began with a trenchant denunciation of the petition reprinted in the *Eagle* from "We, the citizens of this Christian land of liberty" in which he pointed out that the framers had in fact gone out of their way to *avoid* any possibility of a national religion. He also took issue with the characterization of Harding's sermon as "patriotic" advice.

Then he turned to his fellow Jews.

"We have a very large number of people who consider themselves Jews who are afraid of arousing any discussion of their status as Jews and citizens, that they prefer to suffer in ignominious silence any and every assault that may be made upon the liberty of conscience, rather than manfully defend their rights." The use of the phrase "consider themselves Jews" suggests that he was taking aim at his Reform brethren, as was his wont.[9]

The *Hebrew Standard* had no doubt that the Hirschfield-Lucas brief would form the basis for a final, favorable opinion by the local school committee, but the paper turned out to be dead wrong. On March 26, the committee gave Frank F. Harding an early Easter gift: it recommended that all of the charges against him be dismissed.

On the question of *fact*—exactly *what* Harding had said to his students on December 19—the committee chose to believe the principal and the adults over the children, who, it asserted, might have misunderstood or misinterpreted his words. As for the propriety of the singing of hymns, the recitation of the Lord's Prayer, and the display of Christmas trees and sectarian icons in the classrooms, however—most of which Harding had not denied—these were all matters of *policy*. And there was ample precedent for them, as they had been practiced in the public schools for years and certainly dated back to an era before there were significant numbers of Jews in the country. Conveniently reasoning that any ruling they might make to prohibit such observances would apply only to their own district and not to the city as a whole, they punted. They kicked the matter up to the Board of Education, which, if it chose, might opine on it.

It was a setback for Lucas and Hirschfield and the parents who had signed the original petition but was by no means the end of the story. Hirschfield had warned the *Eagle* that if the Board of Education permitted Christian observances to continue in the public schools, the Orthodox Union might take the matter to the courts. It had no intention of letting the matter drop.

The Jewish newspapers were furious. The *Hebrew Standard* asserted that any school principal whose language was liable to be so misinterpreted should be removed for incompetence if for no other reason. To the *American Hebrew*, Harding's practices had been well documented and the committee ought to have invoked the law. The paper also decried the failure of any Protestant organizations to speak out in support of the Jewish position.[10]

Some prominent Jews still wished for Harding to be dressed down, and it was not just the Orthodox. In an editorial in the *American Israelite*, Rabbi Tobias Schanfarber, a Reform rabbi of German extraction from Chicago's first Jewish congregation and a member of the executive committee of the CCAR, condemned the "cowardly spirit" of those Jews who just wanted to let the matter rest and expressed the hope that his Jewish brethren in New York would fight this battle to the bitter end. He asserted that "a horrible example ought to be made of some of these fool teachers who attempt to foist Christianity upon children other than those belonging to the Christian faith."[11]

To the Orthodox Union, however, the fortunes of Frank Fountain Harding and his colleagues were of secondary importance. Lucas even stated publicly that the complainants were not eager to punish him. What was at stake was the issue of sectarian teaching in the public schools, which was what had caused fourteen-year-old Augusta Herbert to speak up in the first place.[12]

7

To Say the Least, Indiscreet

With the issue of religion in the schools very much on people's minds, a discussion was held in the assembly hall of Manhattan's United Charities Building on East Twenty-Second Street, headquarters of many Protestant philanthropies, on the last day of April 1906. Those assembled were to consider how the public school schedule might be adjusted to provide children with a more thorough religious education.[1]

At first blush, the panel sounded like the setup for a barroom joke: a Catholic priest, a rabbi, and Protestant ministers from five denominations holding a spirited discussion about religion. But they had come together that evening to discuss a matter of common interest: a proposal whereby schools would schedule subjects of "relative unimportance" on Wednesday afternoons, freeing up time for those children whose parents approved to attend church or synagogue without loss of standing in school. This was essentially the same idea Reform rabbi Max Heller had mentioned in 1904 when he suggested that a portion of the school day be set aside for denominational instruction. All the participants agreed it was a good idea, and no wonder. Anything that gave them more time to influence the children of their flocks beyond their respective sabbaths was gravy.[2]

Father Thomas F. McMillan of the Church of Saint Paul the Apostle spoke first. "It is our Catholic position," he said, "that religion and morality are inseparably joined. . . . The method suggested will help us to get rid of that absurd, pernicious idea that religion is for Sunday alone and has no place in the business day." He went on to complain that public officials had been forced to assume a position of "brutality" toward religion. Whether he chose the word because it more or less rhymed with "neutrality" is not clear.

David Hummell Greer, the Episcopal bishop of New York, styled himself a staunch supporter of the public schools, which he insisted could not be godless because they employed god-fearing teachers. But in his estimation the schools were not enough. To counter the "seductive evils of our modern life," he declared, the training offered by the public school needed to be supplemented by religious training. The other Protestant clergymen said essentially the same thing.

Like Rabbi Heller, Dr. Henry Pereira Mendes, the president of the Orthodox Union, who had spoken out earlier about the intrusion of Christianity into the schools, was supportive of the proposed arrangement, which some called the "Wednesday movement." He fully agreed with his Christian counterparts that the secular education in the schools lacked what he called the "three R's," by which he meant not the traditional ones, but rather, "reverence, righteousness and responsibility."[3]

The *Hebrew Standard* dug in behind Mendes in an editorial, but the following week a letter-writer to the paper objected. "The Jewish community is fighting everywhere to *eliminate* sectarian teaching in the public schools," he wrote, signing his name simply as "Educator." If Bishop Greer was right about the powerful religious influence being exerted by those schools, he added, "then it is clearly the *reverse* of wise for us to neglect to carefully watch these churchmen. We know how much they love Judaism and Jews, by bitter experience."[4]

A few months later, an interdenominational organization was formed to lobby the board of education for nonsectarian religious instruction. Greer, Mendes, and McMillan were all named to the group, which was to include representatives of Catholic, Episcopalian, Presbyterian, Methodist, and Congregational churches as well as Jewish clergy. But according to Washington's *Evening Star*, the movement had become less about giving students time off to attend their respective houses of worship than about introducing a weekly class on "the great truths that are accepted by all denominations,"

Fig. 15. Rabbi Henry Pereira Mendes, founder and president of the Union of Orthodox Jewish Congregations of America. Wikimedia Commons, en.wikipedia.org/wiki/Henry_Pereira_Mendes#/media/File:The_World's_Parliament_of_Religions_-_an_illustrated_and_popular_story_of_the_World's_First_Parliament_of_Religions,_held_in_Chicago_in_connection_with_the_Columbian_exposition_of_1893_(1893)_(14742262806).jpg.

and a textbook to accompany it that would presumably pass muster with all of them. That effort does not seem to have gone very far, but the concept of "released time"—offsite religious education on public school time—first put in practice in Gary, Indiana, in 1913, eventually did spread to most of the states, New York included.[5]

In the meantime, inveterate multitasker that he was, Lucas was hard at work on yet another project with goals similar to those of his Lower East Side religious classes. Those courses, while successful, were still no match for the well-funded Christian settlement houses that continued to lure Jewish children under what Lucas was convinced were false pretenses. What was needed were *Jewish* centers that could go head-to-head with the likes of the Jacob Riis House and offer recreational activities in addition to classes.[6]

In April, together with Lithuanian-born Max Lubetkin and Russian-born Harry Fischel, both prominent members of the Jewish community, Lucas organized the Jewish Centres Association to set up such institutions in the city. The group began an aggressive campaign for funds, the *Hebrew Standard* asserting that for each dollar raised, the competition—the Christian proselytizers—received at least $100. "The question every New York Jew and, for that matter, every Jewess, should ask himself is: 'Is it not worth five dollars per annum to save some Jewish child from the clutches of perverted and misguided fanatics and bigots?'" the paper asked.[7]

In late summer, the association opened its first center at 272 E. Houston Street on the Lower East Side. Rabbis Mendes and Drachman were in attendance, as was Rabbi Mordecai Kaplan, years before he abandoned orthodoxy and founded the Reconstructionist Judaism movement. Lucas boasted a couple of months later that the new center had already lured many pupils away from several Christian settlement houses. The new facility featured a fully equipped kindergarten; a sewing class; a choral society that sang Jewish hymns and prayers; a boys' club; a girls' club; and a literary circle. All the teachers were volunteers, and a "Young Ladies' and Gentlemen's Auxiliary" had been established. Fundraising proved difficult, however; many Jews did not share Lucas's assessment of the seriousness of the threat posed by the Christian missions, and the program was not ultimately as successful as Lucas's classes.[8]

Organizing Jewish centers—an effort that in any event ran out of money by the end of 1907—did not mean Lucas had taken his eye off the public schools, however. He didn't waste much time lamenting the decision of the district school committee in the Harding case, though; he pinned his hopes on the appeal to the full board of education. He believed the local committee had either ignored, or been unaware of, Superintendent Maxwell's 1903 order, which Lucas himself had caused to be issued, forbidding the very same practices of which it had acquitted Frank Harding. In early April, he wrote to the board requesting that he be heard before it rendered any final decision in the case. And to prepare, in an open letter in the *American Hebrew and Jewish Messenger* he asked all Jewish parents with knowledge of similar transgressions in the public schools to communicate with him.[9]

When the Harding case was referred to the full board of education, it was assigned to the Committee on Elementary Education. That body was under the supervision of fifty-three-year-old Abraham Stern, a New York–born real estate attorney who had attended P.S. 4 on Rivington Street as a child and gone on to earn his law degree at Columbia in 1873. He had been appointed to the board shortly after the five boroughs were consolidated into the City of Greater New York in 1898 and had been an extremely active member, interesting himself in the body's finances, its real estate portfolio, and its governance. He had served on the Committee on Bylaws and Legislation before taking over the elementary school portfolio. And he was already being mentioned as a possible board president.[10]

Stern, who stood five feet two inches tall and had blue eyes and a fair complexion, had never married. His parents, German Jews, had arrived in America from Bavaria a few years before his birth. He was a member of Congregation Rodeph Shalom, which in 1901 had officially joined the Reform movement.

At first blush, the fact that the committee was headed by a Jew might have been taken as an indication that Harding's critics might have an ally on the body. But Stern could not be counted on to champion the interests of Orthodox Russian and Eastern European Jews, who surely made up the majority of the petitioners in the Harding case. He was a member of the Harmonie Club, the most prestigious German Jewish social club in the country. Many of its

Fig. 16. Abraham Stern, German-Jewish chairman of the Committee on Elementary Education of the New York City Board of Education, who disagreed with the Orthodox Union's position on school Christmas celebrations. National Archives.

members found the more recent Jewish arrivals embarrassing, and it was said that the organization's unofficial motto was "more polish and less Polish."[11]

There were five other members of the Committee on Elementary Education, including Henry N. Tifft, the scion of an old New York Presbyterian family, a onetime assistant U.S. attorney and the immediate past president of the full board of education; manufacturer and politician John C. Kelley, the former board vice president; and M. Samuel Stern, a Jewish real estate manager with roots on New York's Lower East Side, who was apparently no relation to the committee chair.

Stern's committee had first heard of the Harding case in January 1906, when it received a petition from Harding supporters—very likely a version of the one printed in the *Brooklyn Daily Eagle* that same month—protesting how the principal was being treated. But it had tabled the matter pending receipt of the results of the District 39 School Committee investigation.[12] During its April 17 meeting, it considered a letter from that committee reporting that Harding had been exonerated as well as one from the Union of Orthodox Congregations asking to be heard before any final action was taken on the matter. It asked the District 39 Committee to forward any evidence against Harding and agreed to hear from the Orthodox Union.[13]

The transcript of the District 39 Committee testimony, together with the briefs submitted by the Orthodox Union and Harding's defense team, arrived the following week, and the committee decided to offer Harding an opportunity to be heard together with Lucas's group. It scheduled formal consideration of the case for four thirty p.m. on May 29.[14]

A veritable "Who's Who" of New York's Jewish clergy and leadership testified on that day. In addition to Lucas, Hirschfield, and Mendes, who represented the Orthodox Union, Reform rabbis Joseph Silverman of Temple Emanu-El and Rudolph Grossman of Congregation Rodeph Sholom, both former officers of the CCAR, also appeared.

Mendes cited the laws and regulations that expressly prohibited the actions of which Principal Harding had been accused and to which he had more or less admitted. Hirschfield recited excerpts from *Gems of Wisdom*, the collection of scriptural quotations from which Harding had read at the assembly. Grossman gave examples of Jewish children affected negatively by Christian religious instruction in the schools, and Silverman recounted how his own daughter had been directed to write a composition about Christmas. Hirschfield did not demand that Harding be punished any more severely than would be necessary to send a signal that what he had done was unacceptable, however. No one was seeking his termination.[15]

Harding himself was a no-show. He merely wrote to the committee stating that his testimony was already on the record and reminded them that they had his telephone number if they wished to hear from him further on any particular point.[16]

Stern's committee decided not to overrule the local board, but nor was it entirely happy with how the matter had been adjudicated. "A careful perusal of the testimony," it found, "convinces us that, while we decide not to interfere with the conclusions of the local Board, the conduct of the principal of this school was, to say the least, indiscreet." It went on, "While there is a conflict as to the precise language used by [Harding] on this occasion, the undisputed testimony shows that he made use of expressions which, especially when spoken to young children, would bear an interpretation of a sectarian character. Especially do we deprecate the remarks by the principal, admittedly made by him to the pupil, 'that if she did not like his remarks, she might leave the room.'" The committee quoted Article IX, Section 4, of the 1894 New York State Constitution, which stated that no public money could be used, directly or indirectly, "in aid or maintenance, other than for examination or inspection, of any school or institution of learning . . . in which any denominational tenet or doctrine is taught." It went on to assert that:

> The public school is a piece of State machinery, supported by public monies for purely temporal ends. It proposes to give a secular education on the grounds of its utility and necessity and tending toward the development of good citizenship in the maintenance of civil government. It does not propose to, and is not permitted to, enter that other field which lies beyond the purview of civil government.
>
> When we consider the magnitude of our public school system, it is possible that occasionally the principles and rules here enumerated are transgressed. Such incidents, we are inclined to believe, result from the emotional character and disposition of the principal and teacher and not from any premeditated intent. We cannot impress too strongly upon principals and teachers the fact that unusual care and discretion be used on all occasions in their schoolwork not to do aught that may be liable to the construction of teaching sectarian doctrines.[17]

Stern's committee proposed to the full board of education that it adopt a short resolution that read, "the Board of Education modifies the report of the local school board in that it cannot 'fully exonerate' the principal, but records its disapproval of his action on this occasion." This was passed by the full board on June 13.[18]

It was a slap on the wrist, at best. And no penalty was imposed.[19]

The *Forverts* considered the decision "a great victory" for the Brownsville Jews, and a *potch in punim*—a slap in the face—to the local school board. But Albert Lucas wasn't wasting time celebrating; he was already looking beyond the win. Within a few days, he put pen to paper to point out the larger questions he believed the board *ought* to have addressed in the context of the case but had chosen to avoid. He believed those issues still needed to be resolved. On June 17, he wrote A. Emerson Palmer, the secretary of the board, to point them out.[20]

Harding had been charged with reciting the Lord's Prayer, Lucas asserted in his letter, and children had been told to assume the posture of Christian prayer. He had admitted that Christmas trees and images of Jesus Christ had been displayed in the school and that a Christmas pageant had been held there. Was the board's failure to mention these in its ruling a signal that it did not object to them? "It is desirable that the attitude of the board on the points should be specifically stated, so that the complaints which are continually being brought to our notice may be prevented in future," Lucas wrote.[21]

And he was just the man to see to it that it was.

8
The Christs Are Murdering Our Babies

Although there were surely overzealous teachers and principals like Frank Harding sprinkled throughout the New York public schools, there never was any systematic, board of education–driven conspiracy to convert Jewish children to Christianity, despite the hymns and celebrations to which Albert Lucas and others in the Jewish community had objected so strenuously. But the authorities were behind other intrusive, paternalistic initiatives. Creating good citizens required attention to body as well as mind, and so when it came to the health of school children, and especially that of the children of immigrants, those in charge of the schools were quite sure they possessed more medical and scientific knowledge than did the students' parents.[1]

Under the common law doctrine *in loco parentis* (in the place of the parent), a child's health and safety were entrusted to schools and teachers. And to protect children—especially ghetto children—from contagious diseases, the authorities introduced routine medical inspections in the New York City public schools in 1897. These were seen as a logical extension of compulsory education, which New York had mandated three years earlier and justified by the commonsense and legal argument that if the state had the right to compel children to attend school, it also bore the responsibility of ensuring that no harm came to them there.

The city hired a corps of medical inspectors under the aegis of the board of health to visit the schools regularly. By 1902, their efforts were augmented by those of a corps of school nurses, who verified vaccinations, treated minor illnesses, and sometimes visited students' homes to check on them, educate their parents, and make referrals to doctors. In that year alone, some eighteen thousand students were diagnosed with infectious diseases and sent home.[2]

By 1905, the examiners had begun to focus on preventative medicine as well, and the physical exams they performed were expanded to diagnose noncontagious diseases, physical defects, and abnormalities. Doctors identified defective teeth and palates, swollen tonsils, substandard vision, trachoma (an eye infection), malnutrition, cardiac and pulmonary disease, and other treatable conditions.

Among the organs examined were the children's adenoids—patches of soft, spongy tissue located behind the palate that inhibit respiration when swollen. Enlarged adenoids were understood to cause children to snore, to cause their teeth to grow crookedly, to make them more susceptible to colds, and to cause earaches, runny noses, and even deafness. "Adenoids often give a child a stupid appearance," a noted physician wrote in 1913, and "often result in *actual* stupidity because the child cannot get enough air." When swollen, they were believed to make children into mouth breathers, and their removal, it was thought, could cure anorexia, mental retardation, nightmares, and even masturbation. While some of these concerns were fanciful, others have stood the test of time.[3]

Parents were sent a notice, typically only in English, that specified whatever problems were discovered by the inspectors and advised to take their children to visit the family physician for treatment. Some could not afford a trip to the doctor, which generally cost about twenty-five cents. For this reason, the school physicians themselves began to treat certain conditions without charge. Parental consent was required for such procedures as adenoid removal, which involved placing a small tool in the child's mouth to keep it open as the doctor severed the organ with a curette—a surgical scraper. Silver nitrate was then applied to cauterize the wound.

In June, 1906, less than a week after the decision in the Harding case—which had done little to soothe Jewish enmity toward the board of education and its paternalistic policies—Dr. Emil Mayer, a laryngologist, visited P.S. 110

Fig. 17. A nurse inspecting the throats of public school children. Luther Halsey Gulick and Leonard P. Ayres, *Medical Inspection of Schools* (New York: Survey Associates, 1917), 148.

at Broome and Cannon Streets at the invitation of Miss Adeline Simpson, the principal. He had come to remove enlarged adenoids from some eighty-one "defective" children who had earned this designation by being truant, "incorrigible," "mentally or physically deficient," or simply "impossible."

Miss Simpson had first suggested to their parents that the children see their doctors or go to the hospital for the procedures, which were simple and not terribly painful. But some could not afford to do this. From those, she had secured written consent for a board of health doctor to perform the procedure, though it was later suggested that because of their limited ability in English, many parents did not really understand what it was that they were signing.[4]

Each operation, which was undertaken without anesthesia, took less than a minute. Though most were completed without incident, there were reports of some children returning home bleeding, with fanciful stories of having had their throats cut.[5]

Such tales percolated through the Jewish Lower East Side for the next week and, like most rumors, became exaggerated in the retelling. According to the *Morgen Zhurnal*, "idle tongues" had spread the lie that some of the children who had undergone the surgery had died. And so, when word went out on June 27 that board of health doctors were once again visiting the schools, frantic parents descended on a dozen or so elementary schools in the ghetto to "rescue" their children. As the paper put it, Jewish women "left their pots boiling and their babies crying and marched to the schools with such noise that it could be heard all the way to Brownsville."

"*Gevalt*! They are killing our children!" one was heard to shriek.

"Eighty-two children killed in Canon Street School!" cried another.

"The Christs are murdering our babies!" screamed a third.

And from a fourth: "*Veyizmir*! With pliers they are tearing out their little souls from their necks! May people tear pieces out of *them*, oh Lord."[6]

At P.S. 37, near the Essex Market, women assailed the school for half an hour. Frustrated by locked doors, they began pulling bricks out of the walls until finally the door opened and a teacher, Mrs. Julia Hamburger, emerged, leading a line of students. The diminutive Jewish woman calmly escorted her charges down the steps to the street and led them in a chorus of "Three Cheers for the Red, White, and Blue" in an effort to calm their parents and prove that no harm had come to them. Unpacified, overwrought mothers grabbed their children and pressed them to their breasts.

"Yossele! Show me! Is your neck intact?" one demanded.

"Berele! Woe to your mama! They didn't kill you?" cried another.

"Serkele! It should have been me instead of you! Let's see what these murderers did to you!"

"Benele! Thank God you are still alive! Here's a handkerchief to stop your bleeding. When we get home, I'll call the doctor."[7]

At P.S. 4 on Rivington Street, whose entire student population save one was Jewish, parents pounded on doors and screamed the names of their children. After one of the mothers broke a window, the principal, Miss Lizzie

E. Rector, decided to let them in to see for themselves that their children were unharmed.

"You can't imagine their excitement," Miss Rector told the *New York Times* later. "They expected to see their sons and daughters dead and covered with blood. One man tore his hair out. When I say this, I am not speaking figuratively. He put both hands to his head, and when he held his hands out there was a bunch of hair in each one." She finally decided that her only recourse was to dismiss the children, most of whom had no idea what was going on.[8]

In front of P.S. 20 at Eldridge and Rivington streets, twenty-four-year-old David Stern was stoking the coals. He scaled a fence and shouted in Yiddish, "Fools, to send your children to American schools! They butcher babies right and left. I can give you the names of many children that have been killed and buried in school cellars." He was soon pulled down by a police detective who understood Yiddish, but as he tried to drag the young man away, the officer was, in turn, attacked by a crowd of women, who tore at his clothes and rained blows on his face.[9]

Outside P.S. 36 at Ninth Street and Avenue C, a board of health physician was attacked by a mob and chased into a nearby drugstore. The pharmacy proved no sanctuary, however; there, a seventeen-year-old boy ordered the doctor to put up his hands and pointed a loaded pistol at him. Fortunately, a policeman was on hand to disarm the boy. But even innocents entirely unconnected to the schools sustained collateral damage. A telephone lineman was beaten insensible on Eighth Street by parents who mistook him for a doctor merely because he had hung a pair of pliers on his belt; it was taken to be a surgical instrument. A police captain attempting to disperse the crowd in front of P.S. 188 at Houston and Manhattan Streets was beaten by a pair of angry mothers. And two reporters, mistaken for doctors for no other reason than that they wore glasses, were pelted with fruit grabbed from pushcarts.[10]

The police on the beat, unable to subdue the crowds, called for backup. Some seventy-five officers were dispatched from six stations and were joined by policemen routinely assigned to the Essex Market Police Court, which was forced to close down. But even these proved unequal to the task of calming all of the terrified parents. There were a few arrests before the children were

Fig. 18. Alarmed parents who believed their children were being injured mobbing East Side schools. Illustration from *New York World*, June 27, 1906.

dismissed and the parents calmed down, finally able to see for themselves that their little ones had not been harmed. Even then, however, three or four patrolmen armed with clubs remained on duty at each East Side school for the rest of the day.

In all, a dozen school principals were forced to order early dismissals. An estimated fifty thousand Jewish mothers, fathers, brothers, and sisters had taken to the streets that morning. And it had taken several hundred patrolmen to bring order to the streets. Although the Jewish East Side was pacified by the end of the day, the next day, June 28, the contagion spread to Little Italy, where several children came to school armed with salt to throw in the eyes of any doctor who made an attempt on their adenoids. And three schools west of the Bowery were mobbed by Italian women, one of whom actually stabbed a school janitor with a stiletto. Here, too, the students were sent home early to quell the agitation.[11]

That same day, the Jewish action shifted to Brooklyn. Despite the fact that both the Yiddish and English papers had made fun of the tumult and explained what had actually happened the day before, Jewish Brownsville parents stormed P.S. 84 and P.S. 125 at Rockaway and Dumont Avenues, yelling wildly that they wanted their children back "before they cut their little throats." The situation echoed that of the previous day in Manhattan in that the police were unable to assert control, innocents were attacked, and doctors, teachers, and principals were berated. Here again, the only thing that worked was to send the children home.[12]

There was no arguing with the fact that the parents who stormed the schools were absolutely petrified, and the *New York World* suggested some possible reasons for the hysteria. Some, it wrote, had been told that removal of the adenoids would render a child mute. Others associated the supposed attack on their children with a pogrom in Bialystok just over a week earlier that, according to the Yiddish papers, which documented the story with grim photos, had resulted in the death of more than eighty innocent Jews. In addition, a rumor was spreading that murdering Jewish children was merely a first step in some sort of plot to massacre all the Jews in the city.[13]

And if not massacring them, then converting them. The *Tribune* made the link between the adenoids issue and the Christmas controversy explicit, counting it among the catalogue of grievances Jews had against the board of education and other city departments.

Trust in government did not come easily to people who had been persecuted by governments in their home countries. Many had come to America to flee harassment, conscription, censorship, expulsions, conversion efforts, and pogroms. They believed things would be better in America, but old prejudices die hard. Confidence in the board of education had taken a drubbing when it permitted Frank Harding to escape punishment for what many believed was clearly illegal proselytizing and when it failed to prohibit Christmas celebrations in the schools. And now there was resentment against the principals for sending home permission slips in English that the parents could not understand, which caused *Die Wahrheit* to grumble that Irish principals had no respect for Jewish parents.[14]

Nor was the board of education the only government agency that was distrusted. The police were deeply resented for attacking Jews in connection with labor strikes, for shaking down pushcart vendors, and especially for wholesale beatings of Jewish women during the kosher meat boycott of 1902, the funeral that same year of Chief Rabbi Jacob Joseph, and the rent strike of 1904. And according to writer Myra Kelly, a former schoolteacher, they also had grievances against the street cleaning department and the fire department, both of which sometimes interfered with their lives in unwelcome ways.[15]

According to the *New York Times* and other papers, the true source of the eruption was "jackleg" physicians—poorly trained doctors who practiced on tenement dwellers—who resented the intrusion of the board of health onto their turf. Also known as "snips" for obvious reasons, such practitioners could demand anywhere from twenty-five to fifty cents for adenoid removal, but the government's physicians were doing it for free. According to this narrative, such doctors sent men into the tenements to knock on doors and incite mothers to hurry to the schools to rescue their children from danger. They had been accused of similar tactics a few years earlier when the board of health began treating children for trachoma.[16]

The Yiddish papers were embarrassed by all that had occurred. The *Morgen Zhurnal* described the behavior of the parents as "more appropriate for wild Indians than for Jews," adding, "instead of laughing we feel like crying for shame." And the *Yidishes Tageblatt* reported that many of the older children were ashamed of their parents' behavior.[17]

The parents did not fare much better in the English-language press. The *New York Tribune* derided the East Side as "a volcano of superstitious ignorance." The *New York Press* remarked that "with such a mob it was hopeless to try to reason." And the *Times* disparaged the mothers for being ready to believe any tale of violence they heard.[18]

But nobody was more embarrassed, or more critical, than the uptown Jews. During the melee, Miss Julia Richman, an American-born Jew of German parentage who was New York's first female district superintendent of schools, was accosted on Norfolk Street by an anxious man who begged

Fig. 19. Julia Richman, an American-born Jewish woman of German parentage who was New York's first female district superintendent of schools. She made many efforts to improve the lives of Russian and Eastern European Jewish immigrants, but her haughtiness toward them was palpable. Bertha Proskauer and Addie R. Altman, *Julia Richman: Two Biographical Appreciations* (New York: Julia Richman High School Association, 1916).

her to help him find his daughter before the poor girl was killed. There was no hint of sympathy in her response to the man, who was clearly terrified, nor did she treat him with much respect. She simply scolded him and told him he should be ashamed of himself.

Nonplussed, the man protested, "Well, you'd care if they were *Christian* children! But because they're *Jews*–"

"I'm a Jewess *myself*," Richman interrupted, "and I am sorry I have to talk this way to a man that speaks English as well as you do."

"You don't *look* it," someone in the crowd observed about Richman, at which point she was pelted with vegetables and stones.

Julia Richman was something of a paradox. She effected many positive changes, both in her official capacity and in her private charitable work. And she had actually left her uptown home and voluntarily taken up residence on the East Side, where she was in charge of two school districts. But despite her efforts to improve the lives of the more recent Russian and

Eastern European immigrants, her haughtiness toward them was palpable. At graduation exercises at P.S. 75 later that same day, she took the opportunity to admonish the Jewish parents present, suggesting that they could use a little education themselves. "These rooms should be emptied of your children for a few months," she scolded, "and you silly mothers sent here for a term or two instead."[19]

It was a good example of the impatience and condescension recent immigrants often felt from the more established Jews, who were sure they knew better about almost everything. The downtowners would shortly see another manifestation of that prejudice as the issue of Christmas celebrations in the public schools continued to play out at the board of education.

9

There Is Nothing Harmful in These Christmas Observances

The Establishment Clause, a passage in the First Amendment to the U.S. Constitution adopted in 1791, states that "Congress shall make no law respecting an establishment of religion or prohibiting the free exercise thereof." But it was not until 1947 that the Supreme Court ruled this provision applicable to state and local governments. So in 1906 the proper place of religion in the public schools was a matter for the forty-five states to decide themselves. New York was thus not the only place in America where it was being debated.

In most states, a provision in either the state constitution or its statutes addressed sectarian instruction in the schools. And while the wording varied—New York's constitution prohibited public money going to any school "in which denominational tenet or doctrine is taught," while others forbade giving preference to any one religious sect, or prohibited religious books from being used in the schools—the upshot was more or less the same, at least in theory.

But not in practice. One problem lay in the definition of "sectarian," and there was plenty of room for ambiguity as to exactly what was meant by the term. When laws were challenged, as they often were, it was up to the state courts to adjudicate the controversies. The result was a hodgepodge of interpretations and decisions that led to pronounced differences among the states as to what was, and what was not, permissible.

The issue had come up on the state level as early as 1854, when a court in Maine ruled against the parents of a child expelled from school for refusing to read from a certain version of the Bible. Sixteen years later, the Cincinnati school board abolished Bible reading and hymn singing in the public schools entirely, and the Ohio Supreme Court determined it was within its rights to do so. In 1884, someone in Iowa challenged mandatory Bible reading, but the state's court of appeals found nothing unconstitutional about it.[1]

In 1898, the Michigan Supreme Court upheld the right of the state to require Bible reading because, in its view, the King James version of the Scriptures counted as classical English literature. Wisconsin's Supreme Court, however, decided the opposite, declaring that "the reading of *any* version of the Holy Bible in the common schools as a textbook . . . is sectarian instruction, and is thereby prohibited."[2]

In an aside that would have been germane to the Harding case had the latter been heard in Wisconsin, that court ruled further that the prohibition was not removed by the fact that any child might leave the room during Bible reading. But even here, Kentucky went the other way when its court of appeals, ruling in 1905 that *no* version of the Bible is sectarian, allowed that anyone who found such readings offensive was not required to remain present for them.[3]

At the end of 1901, a prominent Topeka, Kansas, grain dealer named J. B. Billard threatened legal action against the local board of education after his ten-year-old son was expelled from a public school. Under instructions from his father, the boy had refused to take part in compulsory daily Bible reading and the recitation of the Lord's Prayer, both of which had recently been mandated by the board at the urging of local ministers. Billard's objections garnered national coverage. The lawsuit proved unnecessary, however. The board did not rescind its order, but it voted to make participation in the morning ritual optional.[4]

At its annual meeting in 1902, the National Education Association passed a resolution encouraging the reading of the English Bible, not on religious grounds, but because it was "a masterpiece of literature." This, ironically, earned it brickbats from Josephine K. Henry, a prominent author, teacher, and suffragette and a devout Christian who found it demeaning to *God*. She considered the resolution irreverent and blasphemous because, as she put it, it "sets aside [the Bible's] Divine Author as a lawgiver, and places Him in company with the literati."[5]

Also in 1902, the Nebraska Supreme Court reluctantly reversed a lower court ruling and prohibited Bible reading and the singing of sacred songs in the schools of one of the state's districts, despite the fact that all three of its judges personally sympathized with the earlier decision. Daniel Freeman, an atheist, had sued his district school board to enjoin a local teacher from reading from the King James Bible and leading her students in prayer and in the singing of religious songs. But the *Omaha Daily Bee* assured its readers that the decision was of little import outside the district, because "it is not thought probable that anyone will object in any other district, and the exercises will continue because no protest is likely to be raised." In other words, if nobody balked, it wasn't an issue.[6]

Just a few months after the Harding decision, what was going on in New York spread to nearby New Jersey. In October 1906, German-born rabbi Isaac L. Bril, superintendent of the Hebrew Institute of Hoboken just across the Hudson River from Manhattan and an associate editor of the *Hebrew Standard*, protested the recitation of Christian prayer and the singing of Christmas and Easter hymns in the public schools. Although in America for only two years, he was well aware of New Jersey's school law, which forbade all religious exercises *except* Bible reading and the recitation of the Lord's Prayer in any school receiving public funds.

Bril vehemently opposed this. He insisted that the Hoboken Board of Education stop the practice. "We do not ask for toleration," he wrote in the *Hebrew Standard*. "We demand what is our inalienable right, guaranteed by the Constitution of the United States."[7]

The following month, the board of education in neighboring Newark took the advice of a delegation of local rabbis led by Solomon Foster, the American-born rabbi of the local Orthodox-turned-Reform congregation B'nai Jeshurun. It empowered the school superintendent to excuse Jewish children from participation in religious exercises that did not conform to Jewish teachings.[8]

In the summer of 1906, the CCAR held its annual meeting in Indianapolis. There was much discussion of church and state issues, and Bible reading in the public schools was a major topic. But there were other matters on the minds of the members of the CCAR's newly constituted Committee on Church and State as well.

Chaired by Hungarian-born Rabbi David Lefkowitz of Dayton, Ohio's, Temple B'nai Jeshurun, the committee had on its agenda the effects of the Sunday laws—laws that restricted or banned commercial activities on the Christian Sabbath—on Jewish communities in New Jersey, some members of which were being threatened with prosecution for working on Sundays. It decried "the persistence with which the Sunday observer persecutes the Saturday observer."[9]

There was also the case of twenty-three-year-old Ida F. Cohn, a Buffalo-based, Orthodox Jewish woman who was one of just over a hundred young people who applied for positions as schoolteachers. The process required sitting for a week of examinations in various subject areas like arithmetic, English, history, and art. Once it became clear that the exam period would extend into a Saturday, however, Miss Cohn balked. She explained to the Board of School Examiners that Orthodox Jews like herself were prohibited from doing work on the Jewish Sabbath, and that her conscience would not permit her to take an examination on that day.

The board's proposed solution was not to offer a make-up day, which it felt would give her an unfair advantage over other test takers, but rather to allow her to read the questions and *dictate* the answers to an assistant who would do the writing for her. She initially agreed but changed her mind after consulting her father. The family quickly retained a lawyer who managed to persuade a judge to issue an injunction preventing the board from holding the test on Saturday. In his motion, the attorney argued that the board's policy deprived Miss Cohn of equal protection under the law.

After more than a week, the board succeeded in getting the injunction vacated by another judge. But that jurist's reasoning was disturbing. He cited an earlier decision that held that "the Christian sabbath is one of the civil institutions of the state, and to which the business and duties of life are, by the common law, made to conform and adapt themselves. The same cannot be said of the Jewish sabbath or the day observed by the followers of any other religion." Maintaining that the board had acted within its authority and that only the legislature was empowered to change the policy, it found that there had been no discrimination against Miss Cohn because of her race. Ida Cohn thus failed the test. The CCAR's committee was deeply concerned about the precedent that had been set, which gave the Christian Sabbath pride of place over the Jewish one.[10]

The committee produced a well-researched, carefully reasoned pamphlet called *Why the Bible Should Not Be Read in the Public Schools* to counter what it saw as a calculated and unified effort by many Christian organizations to insinuate Bible reading into schools by clothing it as an essential component of the moral training of future American citizens. It also offered up a tactical guide for Jewish leaders, counseling them to:

- Be alert for the insinuation of rules into board of education manuals that permit principals and teachers, at their discretion, to allow the singing of hymns, the recitation of prayers, and the reading of Scripture. The efforts, it warned, could be as subtle as a little-noticed proposal to change an "or" to an "and."
- Quote state law where it explicitly states that all religious denominations deserve the protection of government.
- Remind local boards that the King James version of the Bible is a translation, and that a translation is essentially an interpretation.[11]

The manual went on to suggest diplomatic—one might say obsequious—language that local Jewish leaders might use to challenge offensive rules and appeal to the broadmindedness of the members of local boards. For example, "I feel sure that . . . you will not allow pride or prejudice to restrain you from correcting what I feel, and I hope you will see, was a mistake." The committee also provided an extensive bibliography of readings on the separation of church and state, including relevant court decisions that local leaders might consult for reference.[12]

Albert Lucas probably agreed with this, and although he was certainly aware of the positions taken by the CCAR and its committee, his contempt for the Reform movement may have been the reason he did not comment publicly about any of it. He was also hard at work on other issues. After officials at the City College of New York penalized Jewish students who were absent on the High Holy Days, he persuaded them to close the school on those days the following year. And as Christmas approached, he did what he could to ratchet up pressure on the New York Board of Education to explain exactly what would, and would not, be permissible in the way of school celebrations.

In late November, he wrote to A. Emerson Palmer, secretary of the board of education, on behalf of the Orthodox Union. The letter read, in part:

> Around Christmas time a practice is very general in the public schools of teachers directing the children and their classes to write compositions upon Christmas. Dr. Joseph Silverman, rabbi of Temple Emanu-El, told the Committee on Elementary Schools that his own daughter had been directed to write such a composition. It is a very common occurrence. This union is strongly of the opinion that sectarian doctrines and practices of every kind, whether Jewish, Christian, Mohammedan, or infidel, should be eliminated from the public school system.[13]

Lucas requested a meeting with the Committee on Elementary Schools, which Chairman Abraham Stern dutifully scheduled for Tuesday, December 11. What the Orthodox Union was after was a definitive stance from the board beyond the general reprimand given to Frank Harding months earlier. "It is our purpose," Lucas told the *Daily People* candidly, "to force an issue in this matter." And they very much wanted it resolved before Christmas.[14]

If Lucas expected an impartial hearing, however, he was likely to be disappointed. Several days before it was to occur, Stern publicly predicted that the protest would be for naught and revealed his own hostility to the Orthodox Union's position. He told the *New York Times*:

> Those behind this protest have started an agitation which will do no good. For a year they have been at us to issue an order prohibiting Christmas observances in the schools, but we have refused and will continue to refuse. I feel certain that these agitators have not the support of the more intelligent Jews of the city.
>
> There is nothing harmful in these Christmas observances. All the principals have been instructed to keep sectarian views out of them.

> They are, however, allowed to draw lessons of morality provided they do this without using sectarian doctrines. As for the singing and compositions, there is nothing harmful in them.[15]

There certainly were differences of opinion among various factions in New York's Jewish community about the wisdom of pursuing the matter; that had been apparent in Brooklyn when it was first taken up by the local school committee. But to frame them as a matter of intelligence was as insulting as it was inaccurate, since Stern's unmistakable implication was that Lucas and his cohorts were merely stupid, unrepresentative agitators. Stern didn't specify exactly whom he was talking about, but if there was disunity, it was not based on intelligence, nor was it between the Orthodox and the Reform camps, which often found themselves at loggerheads on religious questions but were more or less united on this one. Rabbi Mendes confirmed this; he insisted to the *New York Tribune* that same week that there was no daylight between the two factions on the matter, a fact that had been borne out by the serious stance the CCAR had taken on it over the summer.[16]

The truth is, there was *some* daylight. There was no schism between the Orthodox and the Reform *movements*, but there were some dissenting Reform rabbis. Judah Magnes, the highly influential rabbi of Temple Emanu-El, for example, was publicly critical of the campaign. Although the *Morgen Zhurnal* did not cite Magnes by name, it was clear the paper was referring to him when it accused "two reform Jews, one a representative of the board of education and one a rabbi" of hypocrisy. One was Stern, the other Magnes.

In a lengthy editorial, the paper took them to task not for deviating from orthodox doctrine, which was to be expected, but for abandoning what it insisted was a traditional stance of *Reform* Jewry, namely, that Jews must always defend the rights of the weak and protest when the majority tramples the rights of a minority. This, the paper argued, was precisely what people like Magnes and Stern were *not* doing when it came to fellow Jews who needed their support in the struggle to assert their legitimate right for religion-free schools. And in this case, the affected minority included not only Jews, but Catholics and "free thinkers"—skeptics of all religious dogma—who were equally oppressed by the Protestant majority.

Fig. 20. Children in a New York City school classroom holding hands in a circle around a Christmas tree, ca. 1900. New York Public Library.

The paper also put forth the highly questionable argument that this was the perfect time to wage the fight because the Protestants themselves were divided. It cited the case of the Rev. Dr. Algernon Sidney Crapsey, who had run afoul of a bishop and the conservatives in his own Episcopal congregation in Rochester, New York, when he asserted that the virgin birth and resurrection of Jesus belonged to the realm of folklore rather than that of fact.

When he refused to retract his statements, he was put on trial for expounding opinions contrary to the teaching of the church and was defrocked.

Extrapolating from the case, the *Morgen Zhurnal* contended that Crapsey had the support of "a great portion of intelligent Christians" in the country, a dubious conclusion not justified by the facts. It asserted that this weakening support for accepted Christian doctrine offered Jews an unprecedented opportunity to purge the schools of Christian influences, and that it was the duty of Reform Jews to unite with the Orthodox on the issue.[17]

What Stern had likely meant by "more intelligent" Jews were those whose forebears, like his, had immigrated to America earlier and were more established and assimilated than their Russian and Eastern European cousins. They were surely dismayed when they opened their newspapers to headlines like "Don't Like Christmas," "Against Xmas," and "Jews' Anti-Xmas Protest." Stern was talking about Jews like himself and like Julia Richman, the district superintendent who had recently been so vocal over the adenoids issue.

"Christmas is a day of dual significance—religious and national," Richman told the *New York Telegram*. "Its religious significance should be celebrated only in the home and the church, but as a national day it should be observed in the schools. There is no reason why Christmas trees or Christmas exercises should be barred from the schools, provided, of course, that the exercises do not contain any religious features."

"Christmas," she went on to opine, "when observed in its national significance by the public schools, does incalculable good.... I believe Santa Claus is as necessary as the Fairy Godmother we learned about when we were children. Why snatch him from the lives of the little ones in our schools simply because Christmas has a religious significance?"[18]

Once again, it all seemed to hinge on what was meant by "religious" or "sectarian." Neither Stern nor Richman elaborated on exactly *how* one was supposed to keep sectarian influences out of the celebration of a holiday that commemorated the birth of someone only Christians believed—and Jews most assuredly did *not* believe—to be the savior of mankind.

10

Empty Seats in the Jewish Neighborhoods

In the run-up to the December 11 meeting of the school board's Committee on Elementary Schools, a barrage of criticism appeared in the newspapers about the demands of the Jews, and it seemed as if everyone wanted a say in the matter. Popular opinion was mixed, but mostly uncharitable. After all, Christmas evoked strong emotions among many gentiles, and several papers chose to portray the issue as an unjustified Jewish attack on a cherished holiday.

On the morning of the hearing, the *New York Telegram* printed a sampling of the letters it had received on the subject. Some made sense; others were puerile or simply bigoted. Among them:

- "I would like to know whether this country is governed by Hebrews or by a Christian class of people," someone who signed only as "T.R." wrote.
- From Isaac Abraham of East Broadway, a self-identified Orthodox Jew: "Mr. Lucas and his few adherents, while pretending to be Orthodox, are willing to awaken the slumbering fires of race prejudice and subject our people in this country to hatred and persecutions."
- "I.D." of Brooklyn wondered how Christians would feel if the tables were turned. "If the Sultan of Turkey tomorrow were to issue a proclamation saying, 'since the Christians in Turkey are in the minority, therefore all Christian children in Turkey must sing Mohammedan hymns in school, must recite portions of the Koran and be taught the Moslem faith', what

a howl . . . Christians . . . would raise up. Yet is not that just exactly what they want done to the Jewish children of the city? What a difference it makes whose ox is gored!"

- From L. H. Christian: "The laws of our schools should be made to satisfy the majority, which I know is largely in favor of the exercises. I have three sisters attending one of our public schools and I would not like to see them deprived of the Christmas exercises for the sake of the few Hebrews who may be attending that school."
- "When foreigners come here and become American citizens, they should abide by the laws of the country of their adoption and not bring their laws and customs here for us to abide by" wrote someone who used only "An American Woman" for her signature.
- And from John Cady of the Bronx: "I am not a Hebrew, but I feel that the letters written against that race are unjustified. The Hebrews have done and are still doing a great deal for this country and have promoted its interests in many respects. I for one feel that the letters do not show intelligence or true Christian feeling."[1]

Remarkably undeterred by the hostile diatribes, Albert Lucas told the *Brooklyn Times-Union* that he and his colleagues were determined to force the issue. To wit, he accompanied a delegation of about two dozen prominent Jews, mostly rabbis, to a December 11 meeting with the seven-member Committee on Elementary Schools. The very makeup of the group, which included Mendes, Rev. Dr. Joseph Mayer Asher of the traditional congregation B'nai Jeshurun, Reform rabbi Samuel Schulman of Temple Beth-El, and anti-Reform rabbi Bernard Drachman of the Park East Synagogue, made it clear that the Reform and Orthodox establishments were of one mind on the issue.[2]

The *Yidishes Tageblatt* detected "a certain jocular behavior" on the part of Abraham Stern as he convened the committee. Stern's choice of words suggested to the paper's reporter that he didn't take the hearing entirely seriously because he believed it was gratuitous. On several occasions the publication referred to him as a *ma yufis*, a thoroughly derogatory term of biblical origin for a Jew who behaves in servile fashion toward gentiles.

But Stern's attitude did not sway the delegation, for whom the issue under discussion was deadly serious.[3]

British-born Rabbi Asher explained how divisive Christmas exercises were to both students and teachers. They had the effect, he said, of dividing students according to their religion. They also placed Jewish teachers in the untenable position of having to set up Christmas trees in their classrooms and then explain their meaning to their students—a meaning very much opposed to their own beliefs.

Rabbi Schulman, a Russian-born graduate of City College who had trained for the rabbinate in Germany, posed the hypothetical situation of Hanukkah celebrations in schools with large numbers of Jewish children and wondered aloud if Christians would permit them. But Jews themselves didn't want them, he added quickly; all they wanted was schools free of religion.

Rabbi Drachman maintained that it was impossible for Christian ceremonies *not* to influence Jewish children. And Rabbi Mendes, after reading from the New York State Constitution, presented supportive letters from Jewish luminaries like businessmen Jacob Schiff and Cyrus L. Sulzberger, as well as one from Episcopal bishop David Hummell Greer, the latter of whom testified to the fact that the Christmas tree was, indeed, a recognized Christian symbol.[4]

Both the *Tageblatt* and *Die Wahrheit* believed the testimony had made an impression, as the former put it, "even on the cold soul of Mr. Stern." Although he held fast to his belief that putting up Christmas trees and singing Christmas songs could not be equated with Christian proselytizing, he did acknowledge that forcing students to write compositions on Christian themes was forbidden by law, and he asked the delegates if they knew of specific schools in which this was the practice. Lucas explained that although they had no shortage of such evidence, they did not wish to accuse individual teachers or principals, because the battle they were fighting was one of principle. Nor did they wish to make a martyr out of anyone, as they had done, some believed, to Principal Harding of P.S. 144. Lucas offered instead simply to identify the schools and promised a list to Chairman Stern.[5]

The committee took the complaints under advisement and the petitioners were told that the matter would be raised with the full board on December

19. But the body was torn. The members felt as if they were "between two fires," as the *New York Times* put it. Abolishing Christmas exercises would incur the enmity of Christians, but allowing them would enrage Jews. If the *Times* was right, the members of the committee were more concerned with the political ramifications of their decision than about what the law required of them. The paper predicted they would move slowly, and that is exactly what they did. December 19 came and went and nothing happened, foiling Lucas's request for official guidance in advance of the upcoming Christmas holiday. The full board would not meet again until December 26.[6]

To Mendes, Lucas, and Isidore Hirschfield, the board's failure to act all but ensured that it would be business as usual at the public schools at Christmastime, with principals free to do as they pleased. Lucas complained to several newspapers that there were sixteen schools on the Lower East Side with hardly any Christian pupils that were nonetheless preparing to celebrate the holiday. As far as the Orthodox Union and their allies were concerned, the lack of action pushed them into a corner. If the board of education refused to protect Jewish children from being coerced into illegal Christian worship, it would be up to *them* to do it.[7]

On December 21, the three men coauthored a column in the *American Hebrew and Jewish Messenger* in the name of the Orthodox Union urging Jewish parents to direct their children to decline "respectfully but firmly" to participate in any Christmas celebrations in their schools. It also asked that parents inform them of any school in which Christian religious practices took place. And finally, "if the Board of Education shall decide that sectarian instruction or exercises may be introduced," they wrote, "we ask that Jewish children shall be excused, pending our appeal to the legal authority at Albany."[8]

But the board didn't decide anything, including whether Jewish children would be released from the Christmas pageants. And when teachers instructed *all* students to come to school on December 24 in their best clothes to take part in them and made no mention of exceptions for Jewish children, it was the last straw for Lucas and company. They had appealed to the board respectfully and done everything by the book. They had amply demonstrated that the exercises were harmful to Jewish children and contrary to the law, and they had given the body every opportunity to act to ensure that the law was not broken.

It was time to raise the stakes.

Although some of the rabbis favored sending the children to school with instructions to leave just before the Christmas exercises began, the idea of a complete boycott won the day, and on December 23, two of the Yiddish-language papers read by the Russian and Eastern European immigrants, the *Morgen Zhurnal* and the *Yidishes Tageblatt*, issued an urgent plea to the parents of Jewish children who attended the public schools to keep their children home the next day. Borrowing a term from the labor movement, they declared a "general strike."[9]

The *Morgen Zhurnal* reported that many Jewish parents had visited its offices seeking guidance as to what to do the following day. "Nothing will be taught in the schools . . . the day will be dedicated to celebrating Christmas ceremonies with the Jewish children," the editors told the parents. "Your children will therefore not miss anything if they don't go to school. By doing this, you will win much . . . your children will experience the injustice done to them by the school board. And the principals will see that you are people with principles."[10]

The *Tageblatt* was more strident. It discerned a conspiracy on the part of the board of education—and, improbably, by "Jesuit principals"—to insert their religion into the schools. The board, it asserted, "is hiding itself behind false colors." Well aware that they could not legally allow Christmas services in the school, the board members were merely *pretending* that the ceremonies were not religious, the paper insisted.

"When Jews demand that there be no place for religion in the public schools, they are not asking for favors," the *Tageblatt* went on. "They are demanding something already recognized by the founders of our land that is also found in the state constitution. The officials want to wriggle out of their clear duty, and we mustn't allow them to do that. Empty seats in the Jewish neighborhoods will speak more loudly than all the protests," it added.[11]

Both papers pointed out that in years past, when Christmas fell on a Tuesday, the weeklong school vacation usually began the Monday before. Both

שיקט ניט מאנטאג

אייערע קינדער אין סקול

דיא טיטשערס און פרינסיפאלס פון דיא פאבליק סקוהלס האבען געהייסען דיא אידישע קינדער זיך אויספוצ'ען מארגען צו דיא קריסטמעס צערעמאניען.

איין אפיעל צו אידישע עלטערן

Fig. 21. "Don't Send Your Children to School on Monday," read the headline in the Yiddish-language *Morgen Zhurnal*. "The teachers and principals of the public schools have asked the children to dress up for Christmas ceremonies. An appeal to Jewish parents." *Morgen Zhurnal*, December 23, 1906.

found it noteworthy that this year the policy had changed. No one knew for sure whether the change had anything to do with recent Jewish activism against Christmas celebrations in the schools, but the implication was that there might be a link. Both also exhorted the principals and teachers in the Jewish after-school religious schools—the *Talmud Torahs*—to remain open on Monday and to explain to their students why the public school boycott was important.[12]

The *Brooklyn Daily Eagle* managed to get Chairman Stern on the record. He insisted that all school principals had been warned two years earlier to "refrain from having anything of a religious nature, anything approaching a sermon, in their schools." He was likely referring to Superintendent Maxwell's 1903 order, which had been issued at Lucas's request. Stern added that if the rule were broken, the offender would be called before the board of education and "raked over the coals." And in a direct reference to the Harding affair, he recalled that the one person who had "rebelled" the previous year had been "talked to in a manner that he will remember."

But that was as far as Stern and his committee were prepared to go. Although Jewish himself, Stern was an assimilated, Reform Jew unwilling to ban Christmas trees because, like many gentiles, he didn't think of them as religious symbols. And although there were some hymns—like "Holy! Holy! Holy!" for example—to which he acknowledged there were legitimate objections, he said he believed other holiday songs were perfectly appropriate for Jewish children.[13]

Stern had an ally in Rabbi Judah Magnes, who had never been in sympathy with the Orthodox Union's crusade and who publicly criticized those Jews who "would strip Christmas of all its beauty." In an unsubtle dig at Lucas and company, Magnes criticized Jews "who come before the Board of Education and communicate with the papers, and constantly protest against Christian influence." Magnes discerned no danger in Christmas celebrations; in fact, he thought they might give "added importance" to Jewish religious life. He even allowed that there were Jews in America who "silently bring in the trees and the lights" to their own homes, though he didn't exactly praise them. He added, "Peace on earth! Good will to men; glory to God in the highest. Shall not the day come when we, too, shall be able to sing this? Sing it as Jews, as men and women who have something to give to the world. 'Peace on earth, good will to men'. That is a Jewish thought, and as Jews let us regard it."

The *New York Tribune* and several newspapers around the nation published excerpts from Magnes's remarks alongside a sermon by another Reform rabbi, Samuel Schulman of Temple Beth-El, who had been part of the delegation that had appeared before the board of education committee and who categorically disagreed with Magnes. He insisted that Jews who took home Christmas trees had forgotten their own religion.

"As Jews," Schulman opined, "we must, in a dignified, self-poised, thoughtful way, silently protest against beliefs which our conscience forbids us to accept. We must refuse listlessly or frivolously to adopt peculiarly Christian customs."[14]

After others interpreted Magnes's remarks as *favoring* the celebration of Christmas by Jews, he felt compelled to clarify his meaning. In a letter to the *New York Post*, he insisted that he, too, disapproved of Jews celebrating the holiday under the specious plea that it had become devoid of religious meaning.[15]

Plans for the boycott made national news. And locally, on December 23, the day before the school pageants, the *Brooklyn Daily Eagle* predicted that

Figs. 22a & 22b. Reform rabbis Judah Leon Magnes (left) and Samuel Schulman (right), who disagreed publicly about Christmas celebrations in the public schools. Wikimedia Commons, en.wikipedia.org/wiki/Judah_Leon_Magnes#/media/File:Judah_Leon_Magnes.jpg; Wikimedia Commons, upload.wikimedia.org/wikipedia/commons/7/70/Dr._David_Philipson%2C_Dr._Solomon_Schechter%2C_Dr._Cyrus_Alder%2C_Dr._Sam%27l_Schulman_LCCN2014694542.jpg.

attendance would be down by at least half in Brownsville and Williamsburg and in Manhattan's Lower East Side, adding "there is scarcely a school in the five boroughs where the effects of the protest will not be felt." Although one paper suggested that "the Board [of Education] does not regard the agitation as serious," the *New York Sun* knew better. "Some uneasiness is felt among the members of the Board of Education in regard to the annual Christmas celebration to be held in the public schools today," it wrote on the morning of December 24.[16]

If Stern and his board colleagues were now apprehensive about having punted on a request for clarity that the Jewish community had every right to demand of them, they had good reason to be. They would soon have their hand forced.

11

This Is Too Much to Endure, Especially from Jew Rabbis

"All the English newspapers are praising the plan for Jews to declare a strike against the Christian ceremonies and songs in the public schools," the *Morgen Zhurnal* boasted on the morning of December 24. And it went on to declare that those papers stood "in wonderment" at the courage, determination, and solidarity being shown by the Jews in their drive for *kiddush hashem* (literally, "sanctification of the name," that is, the name of God), a loaded term historically reserved for Jews willing to suffer martyrdom rather than submit to forced conversions.

None of that was true, however. The *Times*, the *Tribune*, the *Sun*, and the *Brooklyn Daily Eagle* all covered the call for a boycott, but none of them took a position on it. All they did was quote the vitriol that had appeared in the Yiddish papers. And forced conversions, of course, were hardly at issue.[1]

Many Jewish families did, indeed, answer the call of those newspapers and keep their children home from school on December 24. Estimates varied widely as to exactly how many stayed away, however, and therefore exactly how successful the call for the boycott had been was somewhat in dispute. The *Evening Telegram* contradicted its own headline, "Hebrew Pupils Out in Force at Xmas Season," by asserting that even in heavily Jewish districts, attendance showed no marked falling off. It quoted Julia Richman, who insisted Christmas exercises had been held in all of the schools under her jurisdiction and that all had reported full attendance, a highly dubious claim.[2]

The *Eagle,* never terribly sympathetic to the Jewish campaign even when the matter had been confined to Brooklyn, declared that "the trouble in the public schools of Brooklyn that had been anticipated" as a result of the protests had not materialized because in many schools Christmas exercises were not held. In its survey of the local schools, it reported that principals in many locations, Brownsville included, had ordered that no mention of the holiday be made by the teachers. The paper did not make clear what sort of "trouble" it had been expecting, but it did acknowledge that attendance was down in many schools and that while local police had been placed on alert, there had been no call for their services.[3]

Two Yiddish papers, *Die Wahrheit* and the *Tageblatt,* sent armies of reporters to the elementary schools on the Lower East Side, who reported that many of them were largely empty. P.S. 142 on Attorney Street near Rivington was half empty; at P.S. 62 at Hester and Norfolk Streets only one quarter of its normal complement of students came to school. The *Morgen Zhurnal* wrote that in Brownsville some 50 percent of the children stayed home, and the *Tageblatt* reported that fully 75 percent were absent at P.S. 147 on the edge of Williamsburg.[4]

The *New York Times* estimated that in the twenty-five schools in school districts 2 through 7—all located on the Lower East Side of Manhattan in the area bounded by the East River and the Bowery to the east and west and Canal Street and East Houston Street to the south and north—somewhere between twenty and twenty-five thousand children, about one-third of the school population in the section, remained at home. Most absentees were in the primary grades. Julia Richman's assessment notwithstanding, the consensus was that depending on the school, anywhere between 33 and 60 percent of the children had stayed home. The situation was similar in the Jewish districts of Brooklyn, the *Times* reported, where there was a falling off of between 25 and 50 percent.[5]

The paper also reported that many of the pupils who did attend told their teachers they had been obliged to surmount obstacles to get to school. They told stories of men—sometimes the janitors in their tenements, sometimes total strangers—ordering them back to their homes if they appeared on the street carrying books. And some press reports suggested that many Jewish

Fig. 23. Three-quarters of the students at P.S. 62 at Hester and Norfolk Streets on Manhattan's Lower East Side boycotted classes on December 24, 1906. New York City Department of Records and Information Services.

children had stayed out without their parents' knowledge. By the same token, however, some had actually attended without parental permission to do so.[6]

Furthermore, not all who did show up were cooperative. The *Morgen Zhurnal* reported that in P.S. 31 at Monroe and Gouverneur Streets, one of the teachers began to sing a Christmas song, only to be heckled by her students. They shouted and whistled until she was forced to stop halfway through the music. In another school, students who were told to proceed to the auditorium for the Christmas pageant adamantly refused to leave their seats. The teacher, the paper wrote, initially tried to force them and finally gave up.[7]

The *American Hebrew and Jewish Messenger* was dissatisfied with the whole affair. It wrote:

> The protest against Christmas, however well-intentioned, could scarcely have been carried out in a less satisfactory manner. Either Jewish children were likely to suffer from joining in the recitations of the day or not. If the latter, the protest was unjustified; if the former, more stringent measures should be taken to remove the children from school.

> The threat to do so, by not being carried out, showed either laxity on the part of the parents, or that the protest made in their name was not endorsed by them.[8]

But where the *American Hebrew* saw plenty of room for improvement, two of the Yiddish papers saw victory. "Notwithstanding the fact that the strike hadn't been broadcast widely, notwithstanding the fact that the appeal to Jewish parents was printed only once in the *Yidishes Tageblatt* and the *Morgen Zhurnal*, it still yielded strong results, and today the big shots at the Board of Education find themselves dealing with a power that doesn't allow itself to be trampled," the *Tageblatt* crowed. And to the *Morgen Zhurnal*, the day was a great success because as far as the paper was concerned, Jews had "dealt a death blow to religious ceremonies in the public schools."[9]

There was, however, a good deal of irony in the events of the day, because many of the schools that were boycotted didn't actually *need* boycotting. Some principals of schools with large numbers of Jewish children had been so cowed—or, perhaps, persuaded—by Lucas and company's campaign that they took as much religion as they could out of the celebrations or eliminated them entirely. By failing to give clear instructions, by leaving what was, and what was not, acceptable to the judgment of the principals, and by continuing to insist that there was such a thing as a nonsectarian Christmas celebration, the board of education had ensured that the situation in the public schools on December 24 would be a mixed bag.

At P.S. 2 on Henry Street, for example, the reporters from *Die Wahrheit* saw few signs of sectarianism. All they saw was students playing patriotic songs on the piano and a teacher telling them that Santa Claus was a myth.

"We have always made an effort to make a bit of a holiday for Christmas, but we never have had any Christian ceremonies," the instructor, a Mr. Frost, told the reporters. "We practice no religion in this school. We give a general education and we have nothing to do with religion. Many Jewish parents know me, and know full well that we never demanded, and will never require, religious feelings from our people."

The principal of P.S. 22 at Sheriff and Stanton Streets, a Miss Gold, had taken the boycott very personally. She told the paper that she had given an order a week earlier that there be no Christmas ceremonies at all and that all the children had been told about it. She had therefore expected normal attendance and was upset when fully three-quarters of them failed to show up. "You can't imagine how I feel," she complained to the reporters. "The whole story is a lie. For more than 30 years I've been a teacher in schools in the Jewish neighborhoods, and I can personally vouch for the fact that in *none* of the schools do they celebrate Christmas as a religious holiday."

"I'm telling you," Miss Gold exclaimed bitterly, "that a movement should be started *against* those Jews who incited their brothers not to allow their children to go to school. They are betrayers of their own people. They are among those who are guilty of *increasing* antisemitism. We are trying to cultivate brotherhood among the children; we want to diminish racial hatred. And all of a sudden come people who get in the way of our work."

The principal at P.S. 142 agreed. He asserted that if the rabbis launched an impartial investigation, they would find out that the whole story of learning the Christian religion in the schools is a "lie from morning to night."[10]

Such an impartial investigation, however, would actually have revealed a situation that was very much a mishmash. At P.S. 177 at Market and Monroe Streets, for example, the program was very heavy with hymns and Bible reading, not to mention Christmas trees, holly, stockings, presents, and Santa Claus. And half a dozen schools, according to the *New York Times*, followed an unmistakably sectarian program of exercises:

Song: "Holy Night"
Recitation: "Why Do the Christmas Bells Ring"
Song: "Mighty Jehovah"
Song: "Wake, Christian Children"
Song: "Christ Is Born"[11]

Abraham Stern, derided by *Jewish Outlook* as "the timid Jewish member of the Board of Education," visited several elementary schools on December 24, ostensibly to determine whether there was anything offensive about the Christmas celebrations and judge for himself whether the matter could safely be left to the principals in the future. But what was offensive, of course, was in the eye of the beholder. Stern told the newspapers that in the schools he visited "there was nothing sectarian about the hymns, compositions or decorations used in the celebrations. In the kindergartens the children danced around Christmas trees," he added, and he claimed even to have seen some Jewish mothers help trim the trees. He also put the average falling off in attendance at only fifteen percent.[12]

"I am a member of the Jewish race myself," he told the *New York Tribune*, "But I am not at all in sympathy with the tirade that has been stirred up against Christmas exercises in the schools," he added. "I think the Jewish papers saw a chance to make a sensation."[13]

The *Tageblatt* wrote that Stern "twisted like a snake" when he said this, but *Die Wahrheit*, which had reported on December 23 on the plans for a boycott but had not gone so far as to urge Jewish parents to partake in it, agreed with him. On December 25 it went at its sister papers, the *Tageblatt* and the *Morgen Zhurnal*, with both barrels, blaming them for duping the Jewish community into believing that proselytizing in the schools was a far more serious, systemic problem than it actually was. Apparently its editor, Louis E. Miller, a Russian-Jewish socialist and political activist, had changed his mind about the "vast antisemitic conspiracy" his paper had alleged several months earlier in connection with Principal Harding's conduct, and now believed the embittered teachers and the principals in the downtown schools his reporters had interviewed the day before when they noticed few signs of sectarianism.[14]

"We would be the last ones to brush aside the Jewish mothers and fathers for their boycott yesterday if we truly believed that the Jewish children faced the danger of being influenced to become Christian through these Christian ceremonies and Christian thought," read Miller's editorial. But he dismissed the idea that there was any serious proselytizing going on as "a humbug from beginning to end . . . because it raises the question of race and religious struggle where there are no grounds for it."

The editorial echoed Stern in accusing the other papers of deliberately sensationalizing the issue in order to increase sales. It also pointed out that stirring up the masses was fairly easily accomplished. And it likened the boycott to the commotion raised by Jewish parents the previous June when the rumor circulated that their children's throats were being cut.

The paper did not dismiss the issue out of hand, though. It simply maintained that there was not enough substance to justify a boycott, and that it had been a mistake from the beginning for Jews to take ownership of an issue that was not theirs alone and that ought to have been raised more broadly.[15]

The *Jewish Outlook* thought Stern's unwillingness to take a stand against the exercises stemmed from fear of being accused of showing favoritism to Jews. Although he publicly dismissed the events of the day as "a tempest in a teapot," it was clear he was feeling some heat. After all, none of it would have happened had he kept his promise and brought reasonable recommendations to the full board when he said he would. He told the newspapers that before Christmas he had issued instructions to the principals to avoid any "Christological" celebrations, and he had believed that that would be sufficient. Now he told the *Times* that his committee planned to make a report to the board within two weeks. He explained that they had deliberately delayed action on the issue "to see if the principals could be trusted to keep anything objectionable from their programs," adding, "we have found they are to be trusted."[16]

Stern may have found reason to trust his principals, but Albert Lucas certainly did not. He told the press about a Jewish boy at P.S. 77 in Brooklyn who had been taught a hymn entitled, "Birthday of a King" by the school's vice principal. It began:

In a little village of Bethlehem,
There lay a child one day,
And the sky was bright with a holy light
O'er the place where Jesus lay.[17]

What was worse, Lucas said, was that the boy had apparently been taught the song from a book on the board of education's approved list.[18]

Predictably, some of the criticism of the boycott that appeared in the English-language press was ferociously antisemitic. In an article entitled, "Christ-Killing Jews in America," for example, a Pennsylvania paper took the opportunity to spew as much anti-Jewish bile as it could muster. Suggesting that Jewish people were pagans beholden to Christians for *allowing* them into America in the first place, and asserting that the country had been "founded

Fig. 24. Three Jewish newsboys hawking the Yiddish-language daily *Die Wahrheit*. Library of Congress, tile.loc.gov/storage-services/service/pnp/nclc/03800/03862r.jpg.

on Christ" and that there was something called "the American religion," it spouted the antisemitic canard that it had been Jews who had persecuted and crucified Jesus Christ in biblical times, as if that were germane to the boycott. It went on to complain:

> This Jewish people now are seeking to dictate the manner the New York schools shall be managed. Whenever persecuted and impoverished by

> other nations, the United States has befriended them and taken their part. This friendly spirit has encouraged the rabbis to ask the officials of New York to dethrone Christ in the public schools. This is too much to endure, especially from Jew rabbis.
>
> The American religion is founded upon the eternal truth that Christ is God and God to the world is manifest in the son—Jesus Christ. Not only our religion but our grand public school system, our colleges and our hospitals are founded upon Christ, who is Savior, Mediator, Advocate, Redeemer, to the world. The Jew has no Christ. He calls Him imposter and he wants to renounce Him because his paganism has no Christ. The Jew rabbis have begun the Herculean task of their lives by their indirect attack upon the Christian religion and will fare no better in America than they are now in Russia. The best Jew living would be immeasurably better if dead.[19]

The *Jewish Voice* easily dismissed the piece as the work of a "narrow-minded bigot," but then promptly turned its fire on Lucas and company. "Why give such fellows in the press an opportunity?" it asked rhetorically. "Why awaken the dark fiends of fanaticism? Why arouse the infernal forces when by a simpler process we can keep them silenced forever?" It called on Jews to "work for light in a different way" but made no suggestion as to what that simpler process or that different way might be.[20]

The *Tageblatt* responded to the many critics who portrayed the entire effort as anti-Christmas. Wrapping itself in the flag, the paper insisted that its exhortation to Jewish parents had not been due to opposition to the holiday itself, but was, rather, "merely an *American* way of expressing our disapproval of the *un-American* attitude on the part of the school board," which had evaded the issue. The paper acknowledged that many school principals had indeed dialed back the more religious aspects of the celebrations but asserted that this state of affairs was still unsatisfactory, because it was impossible to celebrate Christmas and ignore its religious significance.[21]

The boycott itself was technically illegal, as unexcused absence from school was against the law. The *Times* made some inquiries with the board of education to determine whether there was any appetite there for prosecuting the parents who had kept their children home and predicted the board would likely let the matter die, which is exactly what happened. Some officials even offered the excuse that not all the absences were necessarily attributable to the boycott; the temperature in New York that day had been only thirteen degrees above zero, and the wind was brisk and biting. It was also the day before a week-long vacation.[22]

The boycott raised the hackles of Protestant groups who sensed a threat in it, just as Jews felt threatened by the Christmas celebrations. None other than Jacob Riis, Albert Lucas's arch nemesis in the settlement house controversy, wrote Jacob Schiff—who had advocated banning Christmas celebrations in the schools but had played no role in the boycott—to urge him to "call off the Jews who are meddling with Christmas." He warned that if Jews questioned the holiday, they would be sorry. "Once that dog is loosed," he wrote, "we shall have trouble as they had abroad and of peace and goodwill there will be an end."[23]

The *Catholic Fortnightly Review* saw the controversy as "another demonstration of the sham and false pretense involved in the idea of non-sectarianism claimed for the public school system," a view with which most Jews would probably have agreed. But ironically, a couple of weeks afterward, the *Jewish Voice* denounced the Catholic paper, not because of the argument itself, but because of the motive it discerned behind it. "We oppose sectarianism in these schools because, with all our heart and soul, we wish them well and would have them perpetuated," it wrote. "Our Catholic brethren oppose them as they would oppose anything which tends toward non-sectarianism and freedom of thought and conscience."[24]

The Catholic Columbian, a weekly publication of the Roman Catholic Diocese of Columbus, Ohio, lamented the idea of Christmas without Christ, but it wrote admiringly of the pluck of the New York Jews:

> There is one thing to be said about our Hebrew neighbors. As soon as they have any strength in a community, they assert themselves—they stand up for what they consider to be their rights, they "kick" against grievances. They are not timid. They are not afraid to show their colors—they are proud to be known as Jews. They get together,

> mass their influence, pursue vindictively those who resist them, and persist in their course until they win.[25]

That was a pretty accurate description of Albert Lucas's style. He paid no mind to the voices, Christian *or* Jewish, that predicted that his crusade would backfire. He still meant to win, and vowed to take the matter to the courts if the board of education didn't step up.[26]

12
Sanctioned by Custom

On January 8, 1907, the full board of education considered a set of recommendations prepared by Abraham Stern's committee for system-wide standards to govern religious celebrations in the public schools.

The document began by recounting the objections raised by the Orthodox Union, and it quoted from the committee's earlier report on the Harding case in which it had asserted that the public school is "a piece of State machinery" that purports to provide a secular education. It then laid out the committee's opinion that the assignment of essays on religious topics and the singing of hymns of a sectarian or denominational character were to be avoided. It suggested that the latter could be circumvented by "the elimination from the list of text-books of all books containing songs or hymns of this character."

It did not, however, take issue with the provision in the bylaws of the board of education that all schools be opened with reading from the Holy Scriptures, despite the fact that it was nearly always the King James translation that was used. It merely took that provision to mean that all *other* works of a religious character, which presumably included *Gems of Wisdom*, the inspirational work chosen by Principal Harding more than a year earlier, were forbidden. As for the Lord's Prayer, which appears in the New Testament, the committee disapproved of "requiring pupils to assume an attitude of prayer" while reciting it but asserted that such instances were so rare that no board action was required on the subject. It did not take issue with recitation of the prayer itself.

The board's bylaws were silent on Christmas celebrations in the schools, and the Stern committee offered a litany of reasons for maintaining the status quo, noting that these were "sanctioned by custom" and that it considered them "unobjectionable." As long as sectarian hymns and allusions to the religious aspects of the holiday were omitted, it wrote, these should continue to be allowed at the discretion of the principals. And as for religious images displayed in the school, the committee members punted, asserting that no evidence for that had been provided, and that they did not believe it was within their purview to specify what sorts of decorations were and were not acceptable.

It offered the full board the following resolutions:

- *Resolved,* that the singing in the public schools of hymns or songs of a sectarian character be forbidden; and that song books containing songs and hymns of this character should be stricken from the list of text-books.
- *Resolved,* that the reading from any distinctive religious treatise or book other than the Bible be forbidden, and that all such books and treatises should be stricken from the text-book list.
- *Resolved,* that assigning to pupils the task of preparing essays or compositions upon any distinctive religious topic be forbidden.
- *Resolved,* that, in holding exercises at the beginning of the winter vacation, great care should be taken to eliminate therefrom any matter of a sectarian or religious character, and that the City Superintendent of Schools issue a circular letter annually cautioning the principals and teaching staff in this respect, and embodying in substance the views herein expressed.[1]

In short, what was recommended was a compromise. Both the *Brooklyn Daily Eagle* and the *New York Times* noted that the Jews had won on two points and lost on two others. If the board went along with its committee, sectarian hymns would not be permitted, nor would compositions on religious subjects. But Christmas trees, holly, and mistletoe would continue to be allowed, as would religious imagery.[2]

The board decided that the resolutions were important enough to require some additional thought and discussion, so it opted to defer a formal vote on them for a month. But no one thought it would ultimately do anything other than accept them all.

The *American Hebrew and Jewish Messenger* found the recommendations, like all compromises, satisfactory in some respects and insufficient in others. It was pleased with the elimination of hymns and sectarian teaching, of course, but puzzled as to why pictures with sacred themes should continue to be allowed. "For young children, visual memories are perhaps the most powerful means of impressing things upon their minds, and pictures of the infant Jesus are really as sectarian as hymns in which his name is recited," the paper warned. On the whole, however, it felt the compromise would probably satisfy most of the protesters.[3]

At the Orthodox Union's annual convention, which was held the day after the Stern committee submitted its recommendations, Lucas asserted that if new standards were *truly* enforced, there would be no further need to pursue the issue. Because Christmas trees would still be permitted, however, and because these could easily *lead* to sectarian observances, he and his committee would continue to monitor the public schools not only in New York but elsewhere in the country. And they would keep up the pressure by sending a letter to each member of the board of education quoting the law governing sectarianism in the schools.[4]

At about the same time, the Reform Jews' Union of American Hebrew Congregations held its twentieth annual council in Atlanta. President Charles Woolner also had something to say about the ruling. He declared, quite incorrectly, that the nonsectarian character of the New York schools "was finally vindicated after a most strenuous contest against the introduction of the Bible in public schools."[5]

It took Albert Lucas a few days to formulate the Orthodox Union's official response to the Stern committee's recommendations, and they suggest that he had become somewhat less mollified by them than he had been initially. In a January 16, 1907, letter to the board of education, which had yet to act on them and which could, in theory, still be moved on the issues, he took umbrage at the finding that Christmas exercises were "unobjectionable," insisting that the exercises were *extremely* objectionable to those he represented. The committee had discounted this view—which it had heard articulated by a broad cross-section of rabbis—and substituted one of its own, essentially denying the possibility that "objectionable" might be in the eye of the beholder.

Then Lucas questioned the committee's blind faith in the judgment of the principals, who would continue to be permitted to conduct Christmas exercises "at their discretion." Citing the fact that some of them had permitted the Lord's Prayer to be recited and others the "Ave Maria" to be sung, Lucas insisted that that confidence was seriously misplaced.

He reminded the board that the Stern committee had asked the Jewish delegation to provide the names of schools in which religious Christmas exercises had been held but had then gone on to submit its final report without waiting for the list. Lucas appended to his letter a catalogue of forty-five schools in Manhattan, twenty-four in Brooklyn, and one in the Bronx in which sectarian exercises had taken place, Christmas trees had been displayed, or religious songs had been taught. This was, to his mind, substantial evidence that the judgment of the principals could *not* be trusted. Further, he took issue with the committee's insinuation that Christmas trees were not controversial by quoting Bishop Greer's comment averring that the tree was a Christian symbol.

The committee's stated reason for not banning Christmas trees was that they "did not form part of the exercises in the Jewish neighborhood." This was demonstrably untrue, and Lucas wasn't about to let the committee get away with it. It also afforded him the opportunity to make a larger point: that classifying schools by the predominant religion of the students was "extreme, illogical, illegal and un-American," and that there should be no difference in the rules governing schools in different neighborhoods or those serving different populations.[6]

Finally, he complained that some principals had attempted to punish pupils for their absence on December 24. He cited P.S. 141 in east Williamsburg, which enrolled about three thousand girls, all but a handful of them Jews. Forty-one out of sixty-three members of the graduating class, all Jewish girls about fourteen years old, had stayed out of school despite warnings from the principal, a Miss Anna M. Olsson. In January, Miss Olsson announced that the entire graduating class would be punished for their disobedience:

there would be no graduation exercises for them at the end of the term. The plucky girls were not deterred, however; they refused to be cowed and decided among themselves to hold the ceremony at a rented hall.[7]

Nor did Lucas stop there. If the rabbis he had brought to lobby the committee had failed to move its members, perhaps hearing from some Christian divines might persuade them. He drafted a petition and invited Christian ministers in Brooklyn to sign it. It read, in part:

> As American citizens, we believe in obedience to the law. Therefore, we endorse the present protest against religious celebrations, services or exercises of any kind in our public schools. We understand that Hebrew citizens request also that the Christmas tree be not permitted in school exercises at Christmastide.
>
> Whatever the Christmas tree was originally, it has come to be associated with Christmastide, and is therefore under the state law, forbidden. The law forbids the support of any school in which the religious doctrines or tenets of any particular Christian, or other religious sect shall be taught, inculcated, or practiced. The Christmas tree now stands as a Christian institute, or symbol, and therefore it stands for Christianity.
>
> The schools are supported by taxation, to which Hebrews contribute. It is unfair and illegal to use funds which partly come from Hebrews, to support schools in which practices distasteful and objectionable to Hebrews are allowed. It is unfair and un-American to make Jewish children attend exercises with features contrary to their religion.
>
> We, therefore, in the interest of true peace and goodwill, and in accordance with the dictates of true American citizenship, which teaches obedience to established law, respectfully request the Board of Education to obey the law, both in letter and in spirit, by forbidding hymns, pictures, recitations, celebrations, Christmas trees, exercises, and everything of a religious character in our public schools.[8]

It is unclear how many, if any, Christian clergymen actually signed Lucas's petition, but one, Dr. Robert Rogers, rector of the Catholic Church of the Good Shepherd, refused and forwarded it to the *Brooklyn Daily Eagle* with his own objections. "I do not approve of the above. I am opposed to it, as a Christian and as an American," he opined. "My own conception of this country is that it is a Christian nation. Its Christianity has been the foundation of its liberty. But while we are offering an asylum of peace and liberty to people of all religions and no religion, and to all sorts and conditions of men, it does not mean that we shall tear down our own fundamental principles and introduce the conditions which the stranger has been glad to flee from in his own land."

Notably, the paper published the petition and the rector's comments under the inflammatory headline, "Jews Ask Clergymen to Attack Christmas."[9]

The full board of education did not take the matter up until February 13, when it essentially approved the recommendations of the Stern committee. The only amendment it made to the committee's report was to drop the phrase "song books containing songs and hymns of this character should be stricken from the list of text-books" from the first resolution. It was not explained why these words were eliminated, nor why essentially the same idea appeared unchanged elsewhere in the resolutions. The provision that "the singing in the public schools of hymns or songs of a sectarian character be forbidden," remained untouched, as did a statement in the body of the committee report that the singing of such hymns could be avoided "by the elimination from the list of text-books of all books containing songs or hymns of this character."

A few days later, Stern's committee requested that two thousand copies of the board's actions be printed for distribution to all principals in the school system. But it fell to the Committee on Text-Books and Supplies to examine all the music books approved for use in the schools. It identified several songs—by one account, about twenty-five of them—that it considered sectarian. So on May 21, it adopted a resolution to direct its sister Committee on Supplies, which was in charge of procurement, to instruct the publishers of all music books—there were some sixty of them approved for use by the board of education—to eliminate such hymns if they wished to continue to supply them to the schools.[10]

For its part, the Committee on Supplies, which considered itself in the purchasing business but not the editing business, refused to do this. It maintained that giving publishers guidance on content was not within its purview, and it bucked the matter to a third group, the Committee on Studies and Text-Books. That body was headed by Nathan S. Jonas, a banker and philanthropist and a Reform Jew of German ancestry who had been appointed to the board in 1902. The mandate put Jonas in an uncomfortable position, because he was well known for his work in local Jewish affairs. His worry, as the *Eagle* put it, was that if it were he who issued such instructions to publishers, it would seem as if he had "made a religious attack."[11]

Jonas therefore also declined to issue the order, insisting that the full board do so as a body, something it never did. But the publishers got the message anyway. They began revisions, by at least one account, of some forty-seven books.[12]

In June, graduation exercises were held at P.S. 144 in Brownsville. They would be the last such exercises overseen by Principal Frank F. Harding. As part of a spate of personnel changes, the board of education announced his transfer to P.S. 11 in the Clinton Hill neighborhood of Brooklyn, a section—surely not coincidentally—in which few Jews lived.

How P.S. 144 parents felt about the transfer depended on which newspaper one read. Both the *Brooklyn Daily Eagle* and the *Brooklyn Standard Union* reported that the P.S. 144 parents were aggrieved. But not so the Jewish papers. The *American Hebrew* proclaimed the transfer "another victory for non-sectarianism." Chicago's *Reform Advocate* happily predicted that in Harding's new position, "he will not be able to try his hand at wrecking the souls of little Jews and Jewesses anymore." And the *Tageblatt* took a victory lap, claiming that Superintendent Maxwell had finally come to realize that the Jewish parents had been right about Harding all along and that whoever took his place would know better than to allow Christianity in the school.[13]

When Albert Lucas reported to the Orthodox Union that same month, he turned his attention to some of his other causes, notably the holding of examinations in colleges and universities on Jewish holidays, the obligation of government entities to excuse absences by Jewish employees on High Holy Days, and his perennial concern, the proselytizing of the Christian missions. He accused several institutions in addition to the Jacob A. Riis Home of egregious "snare and bait" activities designed to draw in Jewish children and decried the lack of organized Jewish efforts to counter them.[14]

But Lucas had pledged to continue to keep a watchful eye on the local public schools, and it wasn't long before another school-related issue required his attention. The new academic year was slated to begin on September 9, which happened to be the day on which the first day of Rosh Hashanah, the two-day Jewish new year holiday, fell that year. Although he knew it might not be possible, he wrote Superintendent Maxwell asking that the opening be postponed by one day so Jewish teachers and students might be excused on one of the most sacred days in the Jewish calendar.

Maxwell's hands were tied, however. The board of education mandated the date and he had no authority to change it. Lucas then reminded Maxwell of his 1903 circular in which he informed all district superintendents that Jewish children should not be punished for missing school on Jewish holidays, nor should they be urged by their teachers to attend on those days. And indeed, the one hundred thousand Jewish students who failed to show up for class on that day were not penalized. It was a minor victory.[15]

Although the board of education had made the decision in February to eliminate sectarian songs from the public schools, if not the books in which they were printed, it took the imminent arrival of Christmas 1907 for public attention to focus on the ban. When Frank R. Rix, the music director of the New York public schools, warned the music teachers on November 20 to avoid *any* hymn or carol in which Christ or Christmas was mentioned, the matter was reported in the *New York Times* the next day and was picked up in newspapers around the country. In the same article it was stated that the song books in use in the public schools were in the process of being revised by the publishers.[16]

The matter set off a veritable firestorm of protest in Christian circles.

13

Anti-Sectarianism Has Gone Mad

"If the Board of Education had manifested some Puritan backbone instead of displaying the cowardice of nervous weaklings in the matter of so-called 'sectarianism' in our public schools, they would not have taken the disgraceful position they have," railed the Rev. Frederick Shannon, pastor of Grace M. E. Church, before a local men's club. "It is an insult to the Christian parents in this city and to their children; it is an insult to the God of Abraham, the Father of our Lord and Savior Jesus Christ."

Rev. Shannon, first out of the box to vent after the *New York Times* article appeared, went on in the same vein, raising the "Christian nation" argument and suggesting that the board of education would have done local Jews a *favor* by Christianizing them. He went on to call for a mass protest by local Christians to force the board to reverse its decision.[1]

Beginning on November 24, 1907, the *Brooklyn Daily Eagle* printed a daily sampling of the letters it received on the subject, all quite negative. From one writer: "If they don't care to have their children hear the Christmas carols in school, let them keep them home." From another: "It would be more becoming the Jew if he would show his appreciation for the favors extended to him, and cease from interfering with the religious beliefs and institutions of the majority of the citizens of a country where he has found asylum." From a third: "Has it got to the point where all American institutions have got to fall in line with the Jews and Jewish ideas?"[2]

On November 26, the *New York Tribune* ran a nasty letter—signed only "Indignant"—that demanded to know exactly how many Jews were on the board of education. But it apparently paled in comparison to the vicious missives from the indignant Christians, and the quotes from Christian ministers, that the *New York Herald* printed. The *Hebrew Standard* found the *Herald* to be "true to its role of a rancorous anti-Semitic agitator" and imagined that it had "converted its editorial rooms into a workshop for the manufacture of letters purporting to represent the feelings of indignant Christians." These letters apparently do not survive, but the *Reform Advocate* also testified to their poisonous nature, accusing the paper of printing column after column of "bigoted rubbish."[3]

Nor was the hue and cry limited to New York. "Anti-sectarianism has gone mad," read an editorial in Michigan's *Flint Journal*. "The beautiful spirit of Christmas time is crushed, and only the tinseled mockery of the Christmas tree and the fabled Santa Claus are spared to dazzle the little ones of the kindergarten." It went on to opine that "antisemitism cannot be kept out of this country if the Jews seek to keep Christ out of the schools at Christmastime."[4]

None of this came close to deterring the indefatigable Albert Lucas. Mindful of the wording of the board's February action, he intended to keep Superintendent Maxwell's feet to the fire. He wrote him inquiring whether he had yet complied with the mandate to issue an annual circular cautioning principals and teachers against sectarian celebrations at Christmastime. Maxwell had not done so, he replied, despite the fact that it was already late November. But he promised that "at the proper time I will comply with the Board of Education."[5]

Various Protestant denominations spoke out, some more heatedly than others. Even the Daughters of the American Revolution weighed in. What was most appalling about this outcry were the underlying assumptions in the statements. That Jews were either not true Americans or were somehow *lesser* Americans—latecomers merely tolerated by earlier-arriving Christians. That Jews ought to be grateful for the "asylum" granted them out of the goodness of Christian hearts and not make waves. That if antisemitism increased as a result of the Jewish protest, Jews would have only themselves to blame.

None of the critics apparently gave serious consideration to the basic question of *principle* being raised by Lucas and company: whether the public schools were, in fact, an appropriate or even a legal venue for Christmas celebrations. They insisted instead on viewing the whole affair as nothing less than a Hebrew attack on Christmas and Christians and a Jewish conspiracy to deprive Christian children of their legitimate rights, and to secularize—or, according to some, to Judaize—the whole country.

The Catholic position was less unified and more nuanced. Board of education member Arthur S. Somers, a Roman Catholic, told the Federation of Catholic Societies of America that he did not believe in any sectarian teaching in the public schools and restated the perennial Catholic position that state aid should be distributed to "every school in the state, public, private or parochial, where children are being taught."

The following month, Irish-born Monsignor Charles McCready of the Church of the Holy Cross allowed that Jews were within their rights to protest Christmas celebrations in the public schools, cheering them on for giving Protestants—who, he insisted, had used the schools for years to oppose the Roman Church—"a taste of their own medicine." But in the next breath, he also accused Jews of trying to stamp out Christianity in New York.[6]

The Rev. William O'Brien Pardow, rector of St. Ignatius Loyola Church, also declared the Jews thoroughly justified in demanding that sectarianism be barred and cited its presence in the public schools as an excellent reason Catholics should turn to parochial schools. But Father Bernard McQuade, the bishop of Rochester, complained that the Jews "have torn the last shred of Christianity from the public schools." He claimed that what they had asked, as the *Herald* put it, "will reduce pupils to clever machines, with no higher aspirations than the getting of wealth."[7]

Nor did the bile come only from Christian writers. The *Eagle* printed one letter from a self-identified American-born Jew who felt the need to apologize for "the views of foreign Hebrews who have not been long enough in this country to know and understand the laws and customs"—as if one had to be foreign-born to object to religion in the schools. He asserted that "the foreign Hebrews want to come to this free country and enjoy all the benefits of Christian law and make all the money they can out of the Christian people and have their children educated in Christian schools and object to any allusion to Christ." A gentile antisemite could hardly have said it better.[8]

It took a non-Jew named J. P. Delaney to remind *Eagle* readers that although many Jewish residents were immigrants, there was nothing foreign about the Jewish presence in America. "Remember that there are Hebrews in this country for over three hundred years. They fought in the American Revolution, in the War of the Rebellion, and took an active part in building up this country. Some people have the idea that all the Hebrews that are in the United States have come here within the last twenty years."[9]

Canon William Sheafe Chase of Brooklyn's Bedford Avenue Episcopal Church, who had weighed in a year earlier in support of Principal Harding, did deal with the legal issues related to the board of education's ban in a fiery sermon on Sunday, November 25, but only to denounce the board for having misinterpreted the city charter. He garnered national publicity in his quibble over the meaning of "sectarianism," insisting that in America it referred *only* to "different parts of Christianity, such as Methodism, Roman Catholicism and Unitarianism, and not to religion in general." He distributed a circular entitled "An Appeal to Patriotic Jews" that was anything but; it was more of a broadside than an appeal and was intended for Christians, not Jews. It accused Jews of demanding that America cease to be Christian and of "destroying our Sunday"—a reference to Jewish opposition to restrictive Sunday laws.[10]

To bolster Canon Chase's claim that Christianity was part of the common law of the state, the appeal cited an 1861 opinion of the Supreme Court of New York (which, despite its name, is not the highest court in the state; it is subordinate to the Court of Appeals) in the case of *Lindenmuller v. People* that was all about the Sunday laws. The plaintiff, convicted of violating them, had challenged their validity, and the court had held that "in this State the sabbath exists as a day of rest by the common law and without the necessity of the State to establish it." This, Chase insisted, was evidence that Christianity deserved pride of place over other religions in New York.[11]

But Chase, who threatened to seek an injunction against the board of education, had an even more odious tactic up his sleeve than a phony appeal to Jews. He had received a letter, he said, from someone named Israel

Fig. 25. Canon William Sheafe Chase, rector of Brooklyn's Bedford Avenue Episcopal Church, who accused Jews of demanding that America cease to be Christian. Library of Congress, National Photo Company Collection, LC-DIG-npcc-25997, www.loc.gov/pictures/item/2016849331/.

Rosenstein, who identified himself as secretary of the "Brownsville Ethical Club of Brooklyn." Neither city directories nor census records from the period have a record of an Israel Rosenstein in Brownsville at the time, nor is there any indication that the "Brownsville Ethical Club" ever existed. The letter had surely been written by a non-Jew whose sole goal was to defame Jews and inflame passions against them.[12]

Chase himself suspected the document was a forgery, but because it served his immediate purpose, he released it to the newspapers anyway, studded as it was with antisemitic canards. It read:

> Don't let your bigotry run away with you. The Jew demands his rights, and the Jew has only made a beginning. This is a free country, and Christians have tried to make it a Christian country. We have now abolished your silly Santa Claus and your idiotic Christmas tree business. Next we will get after your libraries and compel you to throw out that vile

> Shakespeare, who wrote "The Merchant of Venice," with its implied insult on the Jews. You will have to throw out that Walter Scott novel of "Ivanhoe," where the Jew is held up to scorn as a money lender.
>
> Judaism now insists on her rights because Judaism is the real religion. Do you think Judaism has been dormant? Look at your lawyers, your judges, your teachers. Who owns the banks? Who controls the industries? Who are the tradespeople? If the Christians get in a huff and try to undo the action of the Board of Education, the allied Jewish forces can precipitate a fearful financial panic, the outcome of which will be that we will get more than we are at present demanding. In New York City the Jew must be considered.
>
> Keep your Christian hands off the schools. If newspapers uphold you we will withdraw our advertising. Jewish merchants will discharge Christian employees. Mortgages held by Jews on the Christian properties will be foreclosed. Let them beware.[13]

This surely marked the low point in what might have been a good faith debate, but had instead degenerated into race-baiting and mudslinging.

To place maximum pressure on the board, which, if it chose to do so, could rescind its order before Christmas at either its November 27 or December 11 meeting, the Rev. F. Boyd Edwards of the South Congregational Church invited sixteen pastors from local Congregational, Presbyterian, Episcopalian, Baptist, and Methodist denominations to a meeting at the YMCA on November 26, the day before the board was to convene. Other gatherings were hosted by the Brooklyn Methodist Church Society, the Baptist Ministers' Association of Brooklyn, the Brooklyn Congregational Club, and the Brooklyn Presbytery, and a protest on the steps of City Hall in Manhattan was called for. Many resolutions were passed, some with inflammatory rhetoric conjuring up the blood of Christian martyrs and decrying "the elimination of the Christian features of our civic life." These and a multitude of letters from individuals and Christian congregations were all passed along to the board of education.[14]

Magnified by the agitation of the Protestant ministers, the issue struck a nerve with the general public. On the day the board met, the *Brooklyn*

Fig. 26. Nathan S. Jonas, German-Jewish chairman of the Committee on Studies and Text-Books of the New York City Board of Education, who declined to order textbook publishers to remove sectarian hymns. Library of Congress, Bain Collection, LC-DIG-ggbain-36688, www.loc.gov/pictures/item/2014716837/.

Standard Union printed eighteen letters, all but two highly critical of the ruling. Of all the reproaches, however, the one that most stuck in the craw of the board was the allegation that it had specifically banned textbooks containing hymns that mentioned Christ or Christmas.

Because, in the minds of the board members, it hadn't.

It had been the Committee on Text-Books and Supplies that had directed that the publishers be told to eliminate such hymns if they wished to continue to supply the board of education. To be sure, the committee was only making a good faith effort to comply with the Stern committee report language the board had adopted, that the singing of sectarian or denominational hymns could "be avoided by the elimination from the list of text-books of all books containing songs or hymns of this character." But the fact that the board, which was feeling immense pressure, had not *explicitly* ordered a change in the books gave it some wiggle room to assert that its February decision had not changed anything and to insist that it was all a big misunderstanding.

The issue was not on the agenda of the November 27 meeting. The *Eagle* predicted not only that it would be raised, however, but that Nathan S. Jonas, the head of the Committee on Studies and Text-Books, would insist on it.

The paper alleged that some members—it did not name names—wished to make a scapegoat of Jonas. But Jonas had refused to order the publishers to remove sectarian hymns from their books and was not about to sit still for a dressing down.[15]

In fact, there was very little discussion of the matter, and Jonas was not rebuked. There was some drama, however, as several religious leaders—representatives of Baptists, Congregationalists, Methodists, Episcopalians, Catholics, and Jews—sought and were denied permission to speak, causing one of them to threaten legal action. But the board was under no obligation to hear from any of them. As Abraham Stern opined later, not entirely accurately, "the Board of Education is a legislative body. It is a recognized rule among legislative bodies that members only can speak during the deliberations."[16]

Attorney Robert L. Harrison, a member of the board but not of the Stern committee, offered a motion to clarify that "this board did not intend by the passage of said resolutions to abolish Christmas exercises as heretofore conducted in the public schools," and that it had "not directed changes in any books or in any songs." The resolution was adopted without discussion. Joseph E. Cosgrove, a Stern committee member, then added insult to injury with an additional motion to repeal the February order mandating an annual reminder to principals to avoid sectarian celebrations at Christmastime that Albert Lucas had so recently asked Superintendent Maxwell about. This measure also passed easily. Now Maxwell, who had been dragging his feet on it anyway, would not have to send it out after all.[17]

The Harrison resolution as adopted was disingenuous. It was a fact that the board *itself* had not ordered specific changes in any books or songs. But it *had* forbidden the singing "of hymns or songs of a sectarian character" and made no effort to change wording in the Stern report mandating "the elimination from the list of text-books of all books containing songs or hymns of this character." It was in furtherance of this clearly stated ban that the music director had instructed the principals to avoid hymns and carols that mentioned Christ or Christmas.

But according to Cosgrove's reinterpretation, "The object of our resolution was to cause principals and teachers not unnecessarily to injure the feelings of the Hebrews. The Christmas tree, reading of the Bible and the Lord's

Prayer still remain a part of school exercises, and I believe the Christmas programs this year will, in many respects, be the same as in previous years."[18]

Such exercises, apparently, were deemed *necessary* injuries to the feelings of the Hebrews.

In claiming that it had all been a "tempest in a teapot," as one member put it, the board of education had essentially caved to pressure, backtracked from its earlier decision, and hung its own committees out to dry. Canceling the yearly memo reminding principals to steer clear of sectarianism in Christmas exercises—an action Cosgrove artlessly excused on the grounds that it was "an expense and unnecessary"—demonstrates this. The board had now left almost everything to the school principals, declined to give them guidance, and defaulted to an interpretation that allowed for such a thing as Christmas celebrations that somehow did not qualify as sectarian. This despite the fact that to many Jews, other non-Christians, and, indeed, even to many Christians, Christmas *itself* was nothing if not inherently sectarian.[19]

In other words, Frank Harding would be more or less free to deliver something resembling a repeat performance in his new school if he so chose. As the *New York Herald* gleefully put it in its December 25, 1907, edition, "Recent controversy concerning the manner of celebrating Christmas in the public schools had little effect on the observance. In those public schools in which Christmas festivals had been held they were held again. The question was left to the principal of each school. Where principals so decided, an old-time Christmas celebration, with Christmas carols and Santa Claus as conspicuous features, was held." It did add, however, that neither "Christmas" nor "Christ" was mentioned at a couple of Manhattan schools where half the children were Jewish, though carols were sung.[20]

The issue had so aroused local gentiles that the attacks on Jews from Christian pulpits and the barrage of hate-filled letters to the editor continued unabated for several days *after* the board meeting, even though the newspapers reported that nothing had changed as far as trees, hymns, and pageants were concerned, and that principals would essentially be free to do as they wished—that is, define "sectarian" for themselves—without further guidance from the board or anyone else.

Many blamed Lucas for this outpouring of bile, but Lucas blamed the press. He specifically singled out the *New York Herald*'s agitation—which, he claimed, "brought forth an exhibition of bigotry, hatred and insolent malice"—for frightening the board into backtracking, though the *Herald's* voice was only one of many. He chose a Hanukkah celebration at the Pike Street Synagogue, where his religion classes had begun, to speak out on the retrenchment. He bemoaned the "un-American and un-Christian" anti-Jewish bigotry that had appeared in the newspapers. He went over the usual arguments about what federal and state law, and the city charter, said about sectarianism in the schools and how Jews shared pride of place with Christians in American history, noting that "it was not the money of Isabella the Catholic that fitted out the expedition of Columbus, but the money of a Jew."[21]

In one of his more eloquent speeches, Lucas drew a clear distinction between the proselytizing of Christians and the lack of it among Jews, managed a put-down of Abraham Stern and his fellow Jewish representatives on the board, and called for a *second* Christmas boycott:

> We are not ignorant aliens; we are not attempting to force Judaism upon the Christian children, as the proselytizing Christian missionary does upon our children. We neither proselytize, nor bribe, nor cajole the Christian in the desire to show him a better road to salvation than Christianity offers, but we ask that our constitutional rights as citizens in good standing in this country be upheld.
>
> And if the Board of Education, for reasons which it is not my business to analyze, chooses to pander to the vicious un-Americanism of parties who desire to force the public schools into sectarian practices, so that their own inability to fill their churches—to inspire their people to lead clean lives—may be less apparent, then we shall be obliged to repeat an object lesson, which though it necessitates our robbing ourselves of our just rights as it did last year, cannot fail to show our so-called Jewish representatives of the Board of Education, that we and not they, are the leaders of the majority of the Jews in this city. We shall again have to appeal to you, parents of the 160,000 Jewish children attending schools in the city, to keep your children at home on the 24th of December.[22]

The previous February, the consensus had been that the Jews had won on two points: neither sectarian hymns nor compositions on religious subjects would be permitted. Now that victory was trimmed down to only one. But Lucas's exhortation notwithstanding, the American Jewish Committee took no action on the matter at its December 1 meeting, nor did the Board of Jewish Ministers—the group of rabbis from all branches of New York Judaism—which met the following day.[23]

It was now clear that Albert Lucas's zealous campaign had little to show for itself. And that there was simply no appetite for a second boycott.

14

I Will Not Back Down from This

In 1908 Theodore A. Bingham, chief of the New York Police Department, leveled a broadside against the Jewish community in an article published in the *North American Review*, a leading intellectual journal. He accused Jews of being leaders among pickpockets, burglars, arsonists, and highway robbers, and held them responsible for half of the crime in the city. It was an outrageous statement not supported by the facts, and Jews and gentiles alike condemned it in the strongest terms.[1]

Bingham was eventually forced to retract the assertion, but it aroused the ire of the Jewish community. Subsequent criticism of the scattershot way in which local Jews responded to the attack breathed life into an idea that had been under discussion for some time: the need for the broad spectrum of local Jewish organizations in the city to come together in some kind of federation to promote and defend their common interests. In late February of the following year, more than two hundred delegates representing synagogues; mutual benefit societies; charitable organizations; businesses; literary, social, and athletic societies; Zionist groups; rabbis; and cantors assembled to establish what eventually became known as the New York *Kehillah*, a Hebrew word signifying a communal organization.[2]

Reform Rabbi Judah Magnes of Temple Emanu-El presided, and in his opening speech committed the new confederation to taking on both external problems in the relationship of local Jews with the non-Jewish world, and internal problems, most urgently the issue of education of Jewish youth. He urged unity among Reform and Orthodox Jews and the wiping out of the distinction between uptown and downtown Jews. A draft constitution and a slate of candidates for the executive committee was put forward. Among the nominees eventually chosen over the next several meetings were notables like Jacob H. Schiff, Louis Marshall, Rabbi Henry Pereira Mendes, Rabbi Bernard Drachman, and Abraham Abraham. Rabbi Magnes was named the organization's first president.[3]

Albert Lucas was present at the founding. Hoping to dilute the power of Reform Jews in the new federation, he was very vocal about some organizational issues being debated. Given the new Kehillah's emphasis on the education of Jewish youth, an issue on which Lucas had been working assiduously, not to mention his perennial willingness to do battle on behalf of his fellow Jews, he might have been expected to embrace the new entity enthusiastically. But even though he had close friends among the founders, he chose not to play any significant role in the leadership. The principal reason was his antipathy toward the Reform movement and toward Magnes, with whom he had many differences, not the least of which was his vocal opposition to Lucas's crusade to banish Christmas from the schools. Even though some Reform leaders had stood with Lucas in that effort, he did not believe that assimilationist "uptowners" truly appreciated the threat to the future of Judaism in America posed by Christian proselytizing, and he worried that in an alliance with them, little weight would be given to the issue.[4]

The antagonism was mutual, at least among some of the uptowners. After the November 7, 1907, meeting of the New York Board of Education that rolled back much of what Lucas and company had accomplished, the *Reform Advocate* had taken the opportunity to place blame for the board's retrenchment on the shoulders of "our Russian brethren," who, it wrote, "have not yet learned how to wage war for their just rights in the most acceptable fashion." Alarmed by the thrashing Jews had received in the press during the campaign, it had decried the fact that "no truly representative Jew like Louis Marshall had spoken out, leaving it to the likes of Albert Lucas, who despite his laudable work to combat the Christian settlement houses, lacks altogether statesmanlike methods of combat."[5]

Fig. 27. Theodore A. Bingham, chief of the New York Police Department, who wrongfully held Jews responsible for half of the crime in the city. U.S. Army Corps of Engineers.

With the establishment of the Kehillah, there was now an opportunity for such "representative" Jews like Marshall to take on the question of religion in the schools if they chose to do so. The Kehillah's initiatives in the area of education, however, focused almost exclusively on *Jewish* education and what could be done to strengthen it. The leadership thought this was a better way to combat Christian conversion efforts than going after the public schools, and as a result, their policing of the public schools got off to a decidedly anemic start and never amounted to much. As early as 1910, the *Hebrew Standard* asserted that "since the Kehillah took up the question of Christmas exercises in the public schools, this matter has not been handled with the success, albeit without the lack of discretion which it received when Albert Lucas took it in charge."[6]

In his annual report as president of the Kehillah in March 1911, Rabbi Magnes did discuss ongoing efforts to investigate complaints about offensive passages in public school textbooks. He maintained that "these matters have been settled amicably with the Public School Department," sparing the community "public controversy about a distasteful subject." He also committed the Kehillah to examining all the textbooks in use in the schools and reporting to the Board of Education on "any violation of the non-sectarian character of public school instruction."[7]

But this appears to have been the sum total of the Kehillah's efforts via-à-vis the public schools during its brief existence, and even these had apparently ceased before the organization itself disbanded in 1922. After that, years passed and nothing much changed. The hot potato remained where it had been dumped by the board of education: in the laps of the school principals. This, of course, meant that there was no uniform policy; activities varied from school to school, and no further guidance on the matter was forthcoming from the board. Whether the holiday was celebrated at all, and, if it was, what was included in the way of hymns, ceremonies, and symbols remained a hodgepodge.

Without Albert Lucas to carry the torch—after 1914, he turned most of his attention to Palestine relief work with the American Jewish Joint Distribution Committee—any remaining controversy over Christmas trees and carols was very much overshadowed by the related questions of Bible reading and school prayer. Unlike neighboring New Jersey, for example, which had mandated daily reading of at least five verses from the Old Testament without comment and the recitation of the Lord's Prayer (a similar measure in New York that required reading *ten* verses had failed to pass in 1916), New York permitted reading from the Scriptures but did not require it.[8]

Efforts to change that could have been red meat for Lucas, who might have turned his attention to the public schools once again if not for his death in 1923 at the age of 64. Had he lived, he would no doubt have been front and center when attempts were made in Albany every few years to compel

Bible reading, all of them controversial and none of them successful. Various efforts, equally ineffective, were made to outlaw it.[9]

Because the Christmas issue had never been settled in a manner acceptable to many Jews and others, however, it continued to be raised from time to time. In late 1938, for example, in one of his infamous radio addresses, Father Charles E. Coughlin, the antisemitic, Detroit-area Catholic priest and demagogue, condemned Jews in Cleveland, Ohio, and Bridgeport, Connecticut, for their successful lobbying of school authorities to ban "Christmas and Easter practices which embarrass Jewish children" in the public schools. He insisted that such "godlessness" was "the first evidence of communism," and used his opposition to communism as a fig leaf to mask his poisonous hatred of Jews.[10]

The matter reared its head very publicly in New York once again in 1947, courtesy of Isaac Bildersee, an assistant superintendent of schools in charge of two districts in Brooklyn. American-born to Jewish parents who traced their ancestry to Russia, Poland, and Germany, Bildersee had graduated from City College and studied at Columbia's Teachers College before becoming a schoolteacher. He had slowly worked his way up in the school system; by 1925 he had been offered a principalship and in 1946 he was appointed assistant superintendent.

Early in December, in anticipation of the Christmas holiday, Bildersee issued the following order to the principals of the twenty-three schools under his jurisdiction, two-thirds of whose thirty thousand students were Jewish: "Christmas, and other similar occasions, may be celebrated only as seasonal, pre-vacation occurrences. There must not be any reference in dramatizations, songs, or other aspects of the occasion to any religious significance involved. Christmas carols with reference to the Nativity may not be sung, nor may decorations include religious symbols of any faith." Bildersee was aware of the board of education's ruling on the subject forty years earlier, which was still in effect, but he pointed out that it was not always observed. He believed his order was entirely consistent with that ruling and was certain he had complete authority to issue guidance on executing it. He emphasized that it applied only to Christmas carols with religious significance, thus excluding

Fig. 28. Isaac Bildersee, assistant superintendent of schools in charge of two Brooklyn school districts in midcentury who forbade religious references in seasonal celebrations. Wirephoto, AP, *Kansas City Star*, December 6, 1947.

"Hark! The Herald Angels Sing!" but not innocuous songs like "Jingle Bells." He insisted that the order was not anti-Christian or anti-*anything*. On the contrary, he asserted, "it was given in the spirit of seeing to it that what is done does not offend the sensibilities of even one child."

Whether he was aware of the brouhaha that had followed the issuance of the ruling in 1907 is unclear. In any event, he was poised to repeat the mistake of those who had gone before. Challenged over his order, he dug in his heels and told the press that "I will not back down from this." And shortly thereafter, like his predecessors of so many years earlier, he was more or less left in the lurch by his superiors.

First came the by now entirely predictable storm of protest from gentiles. The Knights of Columbus's Catholic Affairs Committee decried the guidance order as "an insult to all Christians" and demanded it be repealed. The

Brooklyn division of the Protestant Council insisted that the nation had been founded "on the basic principles of Christianity." And of course the papers printed a full complement of protests by average citizens, who recycled the same arguments heard in the past. There were, to be sure, also supporters: the American Jewish Congress, the American Civil Liberties Union (ACLU), and the American Federation of Labor all backed Bildersee, as did at least one city councilman. But these were in a distinct minority.

Next came a call for an investigation from Mayor William O'Dwyer. Blindsided by Bildersee's order, O'Dwyer quickly conferred with board of education president Andrew G. Clauson. Like his predecessors of decades earlier, Clauson insisted that the ruling had been misinterpreted, and that relying on the good judgment of the school principals had worked well in the past and would continue to be the guiding principle in the future.

Clauson and Superintendent of Schools Dr. William Jansen at least made a *public* show of support for Bildersee. They attested to their confidence in his good judgment and intentions, and Jansen even insisted Bildersee's order would not be rescinded. But then he proceeded to undermine it completely by stating that it had only been "a reminder of the procedure we have followed in recent years," which it most assuredly had *not* been.

Bildersee's critics were not mollified. "We will not be satisfied with any sort of a general statement by Superintendent Jansen," the executive secretary of the Brooklyn division of the Protestant Council warned the *Brooklyn Daily Eagle*. "The actual directive of Superintendent Bildersee should be revoked."

And that is more or less what happened. Clausen called it "a case of a person overstepping his authority," and it was widely reported in the press that he had countermanded the order. The *Eagle* maintained that Clausen had "figuratively rapped the knuckles" of Bildersee, who insisted he had been correct in his order but had bowed to the will of his superiors. The letters to the editor from outraged Christians continued for a few more days before the matter was forgotten, and the Christmas celebrations in the schools continued as they always had.[11]

15

Almighty God, We Acknowledge Our Dependence upon Thee

Protests of school Christmas programs, often by atheists, continued to occur from time to time, and by the 1950s there were also occasional suggestions of nonsectarian or ecumenical exercises that might embrace joint celebrations of Christmas and Hanukkah. These were opposed by Jewish organizations like the CCAR and never amounted to much. The idea of ecumenism died hard, however, and despite the dubiousness of ever satisfying everybody in a pluralist society, the New York State Board of Regents, which regulated education in the state, got on this train in 1951 when it proposed a nondenominational prayer that might be recited in the public schools by children of all backgrounds.[1]

Concerned that the public schools were not doing enough to promote moral and spiritual values, troubled by a perceived rise in juvenile delinquency, fearful of subversion and the spread of godless communism, and persuaded that "belief in and dependence on God was the very cornerstone" upon which the founding fathers had built the nation, the board of regents decided there was a role for government in the matter of school prayer. The thirteen-member board, which included Protestants, Catholics, and Jews, ginned up a one-sentence prayer they believed would offend no one, giving no thought to atheists or agnostics. It read, "Almighty God, we acknowledge our dependence upon Thee, and we beg Thy blessings upon us, our parents, our teachers and our country." The prayer, intended to be recited at the start of the school day immediately after the Pledge of Allegiance, was approved unanimously, but not, as some had hoped, as a mandate. Local boards of education would be free to adopt it or not, and students who did not wish to recite it would not be compelled to do so.[2]

The idea garnered acceptance in many quarters. Governor Thomas E. Dewey, an Episcopalian, was first to declare his wholehearted support. He was followed by the New York State Association of Judges and Children's Courts, the well-known Methodist clergyman Rev. Norman Vincent Peale, and the editor of the evangelical *Christian Herald*.[3]

By contrast, the ACLU was deeply opposed to the prayer, believing it violated the First Amendment's ban on laws respecting the establishment of religion, which by now the Fourteenth Amendment had rendered binding on all the states. The Liberal Ministers Club of New York also spoke out in opposition.[4]

As far as Catholics were concerned, Msgr. John S. Middleton of the Catholic Archdiocese of New York endorsed the idea of a daily school prayer, even if it was not a Catholic prayer. He issued a statement calling it "unrealistic and undemocratic to insist that the nihilism of the unbeliever overrule the will of most American parents."[5]

Rabbis were mostly against it. Although Rabbi Julius Mark of Reform Temple Emanu-El admitted that the wording "could not possibly be offensive to any Catholic, Protestant or Jew," he and others nonetheless worried that the prayer might be used as a wedge to insert other, more objectionable sectarian additions into the curriculum. That possibility was enough for the Association of Reform Rabbis of New York to oppose the Regents' Prayer, fearing it might lead to serious violations of the traditional separation of church and state. Nor was it only Reform rabbis who objected. Members of the New York Board of Rabbis, who represented Orthodox, Conservative, *and* Reform congregations, were unanimous in their position that adoption of the prayer "would do violence to our religious liberties."[6]

Local school boards in the state, many of which no doubt viewed the Regents' Prayer as a hot potato, were slow to accept it. By late 1952, only a tenth of the state's three thousand school districts had adopted it. By 1954 it had been embraced by the boards of education of some large cities, including Yonkers, Troy, Syracuse, and Rochester. Some New York City schools used it as well, but on recommendation of the city's board of education, others substituted the fourth stanza of the patriotic song *America*, which was arguably even *more* religious. It began, "Our father's God, to thee, author of liberty, to thee we sing" and ended, "Protect us by thy might, Great God, Our King."[7]

At more or less the same time all of this was going on—in the run-up to Christmas, 1951—an atheist named Arthur G. Cromwell of Pultneyville, New York, challenged the legality of Christmas exercises in the nearby local schools. He petitioned the New York State Department of Education to prohibit "religious plays and pageants of a credal nature."

Cromwell, the colorful head of the Rochester Society of Free Thinkers, was accustomed to ruffling feathers. He had been vocal about religion in the schools for years. In 1945, he had managed to close down ostensibly "nondenominational" religion classes taught by Protestant ministers in three Wayne County schools. In his protest to State Commissioner of Education George D. Stoddard, he had provocatively tarred religion as "a chronic disease of the imagination contracted in childhood" that he considered "detrimental to intellectual development." Whether Stoddard, a Methodist-turned-Unitarian, was moved by the rhetoric is unlikely, but he did rule against the schools on state constitutional grounds.[8]

Six years later, after Cromwell sat through a Christmas pageant in a high school in Newark, New York, that he likened to a religious revival, he decided it was time for a new protest to the commissioner of education, an office now occupied by Lewis A. Wilson. He objected not only to religious plays and pageants, but also to nativity scenes decorating classrooms.[9]

He took pains to clarify that he wasn't against Christianity per se, telling the press that he had no more objection to a pageant depicting the birth of Christ than he would to the staging of a scene from Macbeth, and insisting he was not waging a fight between atheism and Christianity, but rather between church and state. To him, the problem was the "religious emotionalism" that was the objective of the school performances.[10]

It did not take long before the predictable backlash occurred. Cromwell received Christmas cards with strongly worded inscriptions such as, "Russia

Fig. 29. Arthur Cromwell, atheist head of the Rochester Society of Free Thinkers, who challenged the legality of Christmas exercises in nearby local schools in midcentury. Personal archives of the McCollum family.

and its satellites is the place for such people (as you) and they should go there and stay where there is no religion, honor or decency," and "this country is too good to even claim you as one of its citizens. . . . You are a mentally sick man."[11]

And then there was the inevitable response from the clergy. The Rev. George W. Cooke of the Epworth Methodist Church offered a veiled threat: "Christmas pageantry is ingrained in the very souls of our American citizenry, and anyone seeking to displace it should be regarded as old Scrooge making a reappearance. Even Stalin wouldn't attempt this in communistic Russia. Organized forces for Christian America will be watching the action of the State Board of Education."[12] This time Cromwell wasn't so successful. In dismissing his plea, State Commissioner of Education Lewis A. Wilson gave the incongruous reply that although it was true that public property was not to be used for instruction in religion, nonetheless "this is a religious nation."[13]

Indeed, it was. This was the era in which the words "under God" were added to the Pledge of Allegiance by an act of a Congress agitated over the Red Scare, and during which there was renewed pressure from Christians to bring religion into the schoolrooms. To counter this effort, which they perceived as a threat, several Reform Jewish organizations, including the Union of American Hebrew Congregations and the CCAR, published a pamphlet decrying "an emerging public-school religion." But it was not notably effective.[14]

When protests were made, the reaction was often swift and ugly. In mid-1957, for example, when, at the request of one of about a dozen sets of Jewish parents in the community, the local school board in Sierra Madre, California, voted to ban nativity plays and New Testament Christmas readings, charges of an "international conspiracy" organized by the anti-Christ were followed by wide distribution of a seven-page antisemitic screed and even two cross burnings on the lawn of one of the board members.[15]

At Christmastime in 1957, residents of Ossining, New York, sought an injunction against the local school board's authorization of the display of a nativity scene in a high school yard. The plaintiffs were not only Jews; in fact, Catholics, Protestants, *and* Jews were arrayed on *both* sides of the issue, and the critics were vilified in an editorial in the *World Telegram and Sun* that called their complaint "nonsense" and that was reprinted in newspapers around the country. They were also, inevitably, accused of attempts "to annihilate Christianity in our democracy." On December 20, their motion to ban display of the crèche because it violated federal and state law was denied in a New York State trial court, which held that the plaintiffs had failed to present evidence of irreparable damage, and that "the constitutional prohibition relating to separation of church and state does not imply an impregnable wall or cleavage completely disassociating one from the other."[16]

The following year, the board of education of the village of New Hyde Park on Long Island actually went so far as to ban the *discussion* of Hanukkah in the local public schools during the holiday season, asserting that "it has no supersedence over countless other religious and historical events and should not be celebrated during the Christmas season in the public schools." Local Jews predictably branded the decision outrageous and discriminatory, but as in times past, the school board quickly shifted the responsibility and empowered the principals to make the call on a case-by-case basis.[17]

In late 1956, New Hyde Park's school board had also authorized, by a 6–1 vote, the posting of an "interdenominational" version of the Ten Commandments in every classroom in the school district, an effort quashed the following year by the State Commissioner of Education, who accused it of stirring up "controversy and bitterness." The complaint, which had come from a local Jewish man named Emanuel M. Belman, had been argued successfully by Leo Pfeffer, an attorney for the American Jewish Congress and the New York Board of Rabbis.[18]

New Hyde Park had also been among the early adopters of the Regents' Prayer. And in 1958, in a lawsuit that would ultimately put an end to all school-sponsored prayer in America's schools, a group of nine parents in that community, including a Jewish man named Steven Engel, challenged the state prayer in court. They sued William J. Vitale, the local school board president, on the grounds that school-sponsored prayer of *any* kind was unconstitutional. When state court rejected the challenge on the grounds that the prayer was voluntary, the plaintiffs took their case to Washington.

In the landmark 1962 case of *Engel v. Vitale,* the U.S. Supreme Court ruled that, voluntary or not, state-sanctioned prayer in public schools violated the Establishment Clause of the First Amendment to the Constitution. "Government in this country should stay out of the business of writing or sanctioning official prayers and leave that purely religious function to the people," Associate Justice Hugo Black wrote in the majority opinion. He also expressed the belief that "a union of government and religion tends to destroy government and to degrade religion." The following year, in the case of *Abington Township v. Schempp,* the court examined statutes requiring Bible reading in schools in Pennsylvania and Maryland and found them unconstitutional as well. The majority opinion, authored by Associate Justice Thomas C. Clark, invalidated daily reading of verses from the Bible and the recitation in unison of the Lord's Prayer. Efforts in Congress to reverse these rulings were unsuccessful.[19]

It is worth noting that although these decisions barred school-sponsored devotional prayer and religious teaching, they did not ban voluntary, individual prayer, nor did they end the academic study of religion or of the Bible. The *Schempp* decision even went so far as to state that "it might well be said that one's education is not complete without a study of comparative religion or the history of religion and its relationship to the advancement of civilization."[20]

In 1971, the court devised a test to determine whether a given piece of legislation violates the Constitution's Establishment Clause. Known as the Lemon test, it took the name of the lead plaintiff in *Lemon v. Kurtzmann*, one of two cases decided together that involved state actions bearing on religion. For a statute to be constitutional, the court found, it needed to have a secular purpose; its primary effect must not be to infringe on, or promote, religion; and it must not result in "excessive government entanglement" with religion. Although the current Supreme Court seems quite comfortable ignoring that test, as it did in *Kennedy v. Bremerton School District*, the 2022 case of the Washington coach who led prayers on the football field, it was employed in the 1980s when the two cases that have dealt directly with Christmas displays on public property were decided.[21]

Although those cases did not involve schools, they remain instructive. In 1984, the court ruled in *Lynch v. Donnelly* that a crèche in a public park in Pawtucket, Rhode Island, did not, as a lower court had ruled, violate the First Amendment, because the government officials who permitted it had a secular purpose in doing so—which Chief Justice Warren Burger asserted was "to celebrate the Holiday and to depict the origins of that Holiday"—and did not intend to endorse a particular religion. By contrast, five years later, in *County of Allegheny v. American Civil Liberties Union*, the court disallowed a nativity scene placed in the county courthouse by a Catholic organization because the county officials who permitted it had associated themselves with the display and their actions had had the effect of an endorsement.[22]

Neither of these cases spoke directly to the constitutionality of school Christmas celebrations, but many boards of education realized that they bore profound implications for them. Some school systems dispensed with the exercises entirely; others made sure to keep them as secular as possible, since it was now reasonably clear that school-sponsored holiday celebrations that included devotional elements like prayers or nativity scenes would likely fail to pass constitutional muster.

Times.

FIVE CENTS

26, 1962.

SUPREME COURT OUTLAWS OFFICIAL SCHOOL PRAYERS IN REGENTS CASE DECISION

Wide Impact Is Foreseen; Churchmen Voice Shock

Edict Is Called a Setback by Christian Clerics— Rabbis Praise It

RULING IS 6 TO

Suit Was Brought

L. I. Parents

Education

2 KEY RULINGS

Merger and Upholds Prosecution of Officers Acting for Companies

Fig. 30. The lead article in the *New York Times* proclaimed the end of school prayer in America. *New York Times*, June 26, 1962.

At the end of 2002, it was Christians who took New York City to court. The previous year, the city's department of education had banned nativity scenes in the public schools as too sectarian but allowed the display of Christmas trees as well as menorahs and Islamic stars and crescents. A Catholic Queens family, aided by the Catholic League for Religious and Civil Rights, an advocacy organization founded in 1973 by a Jesuit priest, asserted that the policy violated the rights of Catholics, rendered them a "second-class religion that would be satisfied with a tree," favored Judaism and Islam, and sent a disapproving message about Christianity. It sought an injunction against the policy.[23]

At a bench trial, the U.S. District Court for the Eastern District of New York found no evidence that the intent of the policy was to denigrate Christianity and decided in favor of the city, as did the Second Circuit U.S. Court of Appeals, which in 2006 did not find any violation of the First Amendment.

And in a one-line order in 2007, the Supreme Court of the United States declined to review the case, allowing the Court of Appeals' decision to stand.[24]

Although he had never pressed for menorahs in the schools, much less Islamic stars, and he could have lived with a regime that kept Christmas trees in the schools, Albert Lucas would probably have welcomed the decision as a partial victory.

It had only taken more than half a century to get there.

16
Not Yet Learned How to Wage War

When the *Reform Advocate* asserted in 1907 that "our Russian brethren" had mishandled the whole issue of sectarianism in the public schools and disparaged Albert Lucas for his lack of understanding of "statesmanlike methods of combat," despite the odiousness of its criticism of Lucas, who wasn't even of Russian extraction, it raised some provocative questions.[1]

Had he and the Orthodox Union erred in their approach? Had they been wrong to take on Harding and press the board of education to ban—or at least set clear limits on—Christmas celebrations in the schools? Had the boycott been a mistake? It was certainly the case that, for all their efforts, they had, in the short term at least, accomplished little apart from fanning the flames of antisemitism. Might another strategy—a more "statesmanlike" approach—have been more successful? Perhaps one spearheaded, as the *Reform Advocate* suggested, by an established, uptown Jew like Louis Marshall, a prominent, American-born attorney of German-Jewish extraction and publisher of the progressive daily, *Di Yidishe Velt*?

Looking back over the controversy, it appears to have been mostly a case of people talking past one another. Lucas and company wished to fight a battle over the *law*, and they believed, with good reason, that they had the New York State Constitution and the New York City Charter squarely on their side, not to mention the regulations of the board of education itself. The opposition, by contrast, relied primarily on condescension, patriotism, racism, traditionalism, and outright falsehoods, and mostly danced around the legal questions.

A review of the various arguments used to oppose Lucas makes this clear. Rev. William Sheafe Chase's oblique reference to "some people in this country who do not clearly understand the nature of the religious freedom" and Abraham Stern's implication that Lucas and his supporters were unintelligent were both simply patronizing. They were designed to undermine their opponents' case not on its merits, but by belittling the advocates personally.

Others, like the Brooklyn petitioners who praised Principal Harding for his "patriotic advice" to the children in his school, the pastor who warned of the danger of letting "Mohammedans and Jews dictate to us how our children should be taught," and the one who lamented the lack of "Puritan backbone" on the part of the Board of Education were simply attempting to obfuscate the issue by conflating Christianity with patriotism and wrapping it in the American flag.

Many were out-and-out racist, such as those who suggested Jews had been allowed in America only out of the beneficence of Christians, and that as newcomers they ought to show gratitude for their asylum and not make waves, lest they be responsible for bringing a flood of antisemitism upon themselves from otherwise fair-minded Christians. These arguments were ahistorical canards on the one hand and bald-faced attempts to intimidate the opposition on the other.

And some of the criticism was simply based on untruths, such as the oft-cited fiction that America was a Christian country and had been founded as such, that the Bible was not a sectarian book, or that Jews were trying to "stamp out" Christianity in New York. All were designed to obfuscate the issue by means of out-and-out falsehoods.

The Brooklyn Presbytery, which contemplated with fear "the elimination of the Christian features of our civic life," accused Jews of trying to upend a longstanding practice. That much was true. But the criticism was based on the assumption that because Christmas had been celebrated in the schools in the past when nobody objected to it, it remained the right of Christians to continue such a tradition in perpetuity, no matter what the growing number of non-Christian citizens might think of it.[2]

The argument that Christmas exercises were traditional, and that Jews were attempting to upend a historical practice was valid, but it sidestepped the main issue Lucas and company were raising. What was missing were convincing arguments about how Christmas exercises in the schools were somehow *consonant* with the prohibition in the state constitution against public money going to any school "in which denominational tenet or doctrine is taught" or the provision in New York City's charter that prohibited funding schools "in which the religious doctrines or tenets of any particular Christian or other religious sect shall be taught, implicated or practiced."

Put another way, to have argued that the laws as written actually *allowed* for prayer, religious icons, and religious hymns in the public schools would have required true legal gymnastics, and most did not attempt it, especially when emotional arguments, however irrelevant, seemed sufficient to make their case.

Canon Chase did attempt a legal argument of sorts when he claimed that Christianity deserved pride of place over other faiths because it was recognized in common law, and that the term "sectarian" referred only to sects *within* Christianity. Neither position was entirely without historical foundation, but neither was germane. The assertion that Christianity was part of the common law was frequently made in the nineteenth century, often in cases in which people were prosecuted for blasphemy. But the doctrine had fallen into disuse by the turn of the twentieth century and in any case been superseded by statutory law. And as far as the meaning of the word "sectarian" was concerned, before America had significant numbers of non-Christians the term had indeed often been understood to refer to Christian sects. But its broader meaning was very much in use by the turn of the century. Even so, Canon Chase's argument was trumped by the prohibition in the New York City Charter against public funding of "any particular Christian *or other* religious sect" (emphasis mine).[3]

As a practical matter, no matter how much Lucas and company wished to fight a battle over the law, the outcome was always going to be decided by politics, since those in a position to rule on it, whether elected or appointed, did not wish to take heat from their own constituencies. To make things even more difficult, their supporters simply did not regard Christmas celebrations as in any way akin to proselytizing. If Lucas could not sway public opinion in his majority-Christian country, he was not going to win a political argument.

Given this, was Lucas wrong to make so much noise? He may not initially have predicted the vehemence of the pushback he provoked when he first raised the issue. But it became all too clear quite early in his crusade that most of Christian America, or at least Protestant America, were perfectly happy with Christmas pageants in their schools, did not see them as a problem, were passionate about keeping them there, and felt quite ill-used by what appeared to be Jewish upstarts making waves.

Yet Lucas pressed on, seemingly in denial about how quixotic his quest really was. Perhaps he told himself it would be difficult to name a contentious public issue that ever got resolved *without* a fuss, and without making the protesters unpopular, at least in some quarters. It certainly appears as if he was so utterly convinced that his cause was righteous and that the law was on his side that he persuaded himself that victory was assured, or at least within reach.

For better or worse, Lucas did make the concerns of many local Jews impossible to ignore, and had it not been for his activism, it is doubtful anyone in authority would have given the issue a second thought. But because he purported to be speaking for the Jewish community, the opprobrium he engendered was directed at *all* Jews, not just at himself. When all was said and done, it is doubtful that he advanced his cherished cause of making America safer for Jews. To some minds, he had done precisely the opposite.

There were certainly things he could have done better. At the beginning of the fight, for example, Lucas clearly overplayed his hand when he equated the public schools with the mission houses and imagined a conspiracy within them to "break down the religious observance of the Jewish children of the East Side," à la Jacob Riis. He had not always believed this; in 1903 he had found Superintendent of Schools William Henry Maxwell sincere in his stated willingness to keep religion out of the schools and had said so.

By 1905, however, he no longer made room for the possibility that what was going on in the schools, though unwelcome and condescending, actually fell short of proselytizing. It had surely been a mistake to extrapolate from the misdeeds of Frank Harding and accuse the entire system of nefarious intent.

Fig. 31. Rebecca and Albert Lucas in Venice in 1920.
American Jewish Joint Distribution Committee Archives.

Harding was simply a zealous Christian who had overstepped his bounds, as the board of education ultimately concluded, and Lucas and company should never have alleged that he was "systematically Christianizing" children or demanded that he be terminated. Despite articles like the one that appeared in *Frank Leslie's Weekly*, replete with pictures of "benighted"—read, Jewish—students being initiated in their classrooms into the magic that was Christmas, the board of education, unlike the Christian missions, had never been on a crusade for converts, nor would its Jewish members, however unsympathetic they might have been to Lucas's crusade, likely have sat still for it if it had.[4]

Nor was the boycott itself an unmitigated success, since significant numbers of Jews failed to honor it and the principals of many of the schools whose students stayed home had not planned sectarian exercises in the first place. It certainly *was* effective in attracting attention to a cause the board of education would have much preferred to ignore, and it did get results, after a fashion. It was covered in newspapers throughout the country and it inspired Jews elsewhere to fight sectarianism in their local schools. And it compelled the Committee on Elementary Education, which had punted on the matter, to clarify the rules for Christmas celebrations. But those rules turned out to be far short of what Lucas and company had sought, or believed they deserved. The results, ultimately, were meager.

One reason many Protestant ministers opposed the Jews so vehemently may have been that the churches, challenged as always in their battle for the souls of young people, were not about to give up willingly a second bite at the apple—the first being Sunday services in church—that allowing religious instruction during school hours afforded. Hence the warm welcome they gave to the concept of "released time"—time off from school for pupils to attend their respective houses of worship. The Jewish community was divided on the subject; some rabbis opposed anything that blurred the line between school time and worship time, but others, concerned that many Jewish children were getting no religious education at all, spoke out in support of it.[5]

Released time that entailed religious instruction on school property was held unconstitutional by the Supreme Court in 1948 in the case of *McCollum v. Board of Education*, filed in Illinois by Vashti McCollum (not coincidentally the daughter of New York atheist Arthur G. Cromwell of the Rochester Society of Free Thinkers). But such instruction was explicitly permitted four years later as long as it was off school grounds and did not involve the expenditure of public funds. Even today, some ten percent of teenagers in public schools participate in it. Regardless of the grandiose rhetoric in which the ministers couched their arguments for this arrangement, many were simply fighting to preserve a tactical advantage. Most of the Jews, on the other hand, were fighting for a principle. And though they believed the law was on their side, the politics were not.[6]

Would the results have been different had a luminary like Louis Marshall led the charge? Marshall, one of the founders of the American Jewish Committee, or someone of similar stature would surely have had better access than Albert Lucas to those in the political firmament. But whether he would have been able to secure a better outcome is dubious. Asking public officials to make decisions deeply unpopular with their constituents is always dicey business, and the skittish New York Board of Education was clearly hypersensitive to public opinion.

The board had been amenable to nibbling around the edges of longstanding custom to appease the growing Jewish community with sops like banning sectarian hymns and essays with religious themes, but it had never been willing to entertain a wholesale ban on celebrations. And once board members came under pressure for doing what little they *had* done, they lied about it, blamed their subordinates, and partially reversed themselves. Would Louis Marshall have been able to prevent this? It seems unlikely.

Though Albert Lucas might not have enjoyed the access someone like Marshall had, there was nothing socially unacceptable or embarrassing about him, as the *Reform Advocate* had implied. The British-born Lucas had a superb command of the English language and was a skilled debater. If he spoke with an accent at all, it was British, not Yiddish. Although many of the Orthodox Jews he represented were greenhorns from Russia unschooled in the ways of America, criticizing *him* for being unstatesmanlike was unfair and inaccurate. He was certainly a zealot, but for the most part he played by the rules, taking the issue in orderly fashion first to the local school board in Brooklyn and then to the New York Board of Education, and engaging with the superintendent of schools. He also wrote many articulate, well-reasoned newspaper columns on the subject. Only the boycott itself was an extreme measure, undertaken out of desperation when nothing else seemed to work.

The truth is, banishing Christmas celebrations from the schools entirely, despite the strong legal arguments marshaled to support it, was essentially a fool's errand. Whether Lucas had changed tactics or someone else had spearheaded the effort, the result would very likely have been the same.

Why did it take until the middle of the twentieth century for school-sponsored prayer and Bible reading to be banned from the public schools? Ridding public schools of Christian influences was an issue that had always had a better chance in the courts than it did with civil servants because it involved defending the rights of minorities. Results in the various state courts that considered aspects of it were a mixed bag in the early part of the century; the rulings often, though not always, favored the status quo.

When the two landmark cases—*Engel v. Vitale* and *Abington Township v. Schempp*—were heard in midcentury, it was before an activist Supreme Court under Chief Justice Earl Warren that was highly attuned to civil liberties, minority rights, and violations of them. It was a time of major social and political change and jurists who took an expansive view of individual rights held sway. The Warren Court made rulings in several such areas that would hardly have been thinkable earlier in the century.

But while dispensing with devotional Bible reading and prayer in the schools had implications for Christmas celebrations, those two Supreme Court decisions proved little match for school Christmas programs, which have persisted. If such activities were somehow stripped of their *religious* aspects, they were understood to be permissible. As a practical matter, sectarian or otherwise, they still went on, especially in localities with few Jews or other religious minorities to object to them, and undoubtedly still do.

A 1965 survey in Iowa revealed that even after *Engle v. Vitale* and *Abington Township v. Schempp*, fully 79 percent of local schools continued to sponsor observances of religious festivals. The Anti-Defamation League found a decade later that in schools in the thirty-one states it surveyed, almost 92 percent still conducted holiday concerts with religious content, nearly all of it Christian. And more recently, a 2018 Rasmussen poll found that 74 percent of American adults believe that Christmas *should* be celebrated in the public schools; only 14 percent disagreed.[7]

The landscape, apparently, has not changed much since 1906.

Afterword

In October 1956, six years before *Engel v. Vitale* was decided, the American Jewish Committee distributed a memorandum entitled "Dealing with the Christmas Observance in the Public Schools." It consisted of a series of recommendations to Jewish communities on how to handle school pageants, which of course continued to be an issue in many localities.

It is "unrealistic to expect the observance can be eliminated from the school program," the report began. "Those who are determined to achieve that end, however understandable their motives, are likely to embroil the Jewish population in serious conflict with its Christian neighbors." In what might have been a nod to 1906, it noted that there was a history of such tense situations.

Among the practical tips the committee offered was to avoid bringing the matter up just before the Christmas season, when the atmosphere is typically highly charged. It urged broad consultation within a local Jewish community before taking a position and going to great lengths to avoid the prospect of "self-appointed spokesmen" randomly voicing their personal opinions publicly.

If a decision *were* made to take "remedial steps," the committee suggested quiet conversations with the superintendent of schools, warning that the utmost caution had to be employed lest the official feel compelled to raise the matter with the board of education and it become a matter for public debate. It actively discouraged any sort of community-wide approach for this reason. It also opposed the idea of joint Christmas-Hanukkah celebrations.

The committee counseled a low-key, year-round approach that emphasized educating school personnel, Christian clergy, and others, but it had no advice to offer if the situation exploded. "If community tensions should develop, we know of no ready solution," it confessed. "Experience has shown that public statements, however eloquently phrased, are likely to have little or no quieting effect."[1]

That memorandum is instructive in many ways. It testifies to the fact that public school Christmas pageants remained a concern of American Jews half a century after Albert Lucas's fight, something an editor at *Look* magazine confirmed when he asserted that "the annual battles over Christmas observances in the public schools are still more certain than snow on December 25." But what the American Jewish Committee was now advocating was a far cry from Lucas's no-holds-barred approach; it sounded more like walking on eggshells. And the committee appears to have accepted the argument, raised by many Christians and some Jews, that if Jews pressed the issue they would only stoke the fires of antisemitism.[2]

Today, there is no sign on the American Jewish Committee's website of even the baby steps it recommended in 1956. Guidance on how to *protest* Christmas celebrations in the public schools is in short supply, both from the major Jewish organizations like the committee and from other groups dedicated to advancing civil liberties. Rather, most of what one discovers on the internet are guidelines for the inevitable celebrations, not tactics aimed at eliminating them.

In late 2021, for example, the Anti-Defamation League (ADL) published principles designed to help school administrators and teachers plan their holiday celebrations. The ADL warned them against appearing to favor one faith over another or religion over nonreligion; cautioned them against activities that "may be legally permissible" but were not "inclusive"; advised them to ensure that school events, assemblies, concerts, and programs "be designed to further a secular and objective program of education," and counseled them to avoid religious symbols in their seasonal decorations. Absent from the document was any mention of how parents might protest violations of these principles, much less how they might challenge the overall propriety or legality of Christmas celebrations in the public schools.[3]

The American Jewish Congress was especially vocal about the legal issues in midcentury. In 1946, the organization asserted that "the observance of the day which marks the birth of the Savior is nothing and can be nothing but a Christian religious holiday," and in the immediate aftermath of *Engel v. Vitale* and *Abington Township v. Schempp* it charged that public school Christmas and Hanukkah celebrations were "a violation of religious freedom and the traditional American principle of separation of church and state as contained in the First Amendment."[4]

But there is no sign of such an unequivocal position on its website today.

What has changed? One might argue that there have been several significant changes: in American Jews themselves, in American Christians, in the legal environment, and in Christmas itself, or at least the way in which it is celebrated in America. And that these might account for the apparent reluctance to continue Lucas's crusade.

First of all, Jews in America are far more assimilated than they were a century ago. Forty-two percent of married Jewish respondents to a Pew Research Center study in 2020 indicated they were wed to non-Jews. Only some 9 percent currently consider themselves Orthodox. More than half belong to the Reform and Conservative movements, and one-third does not identify with any particular branch and may feel "culturally" Jewish rather than religiously so. Fully 53 percent of American Jews say religion is "not too" or "not at all" important to them personally. Being Jewish is about many things, but today's American Jews are more likely to say that for them, it is more about culture and ancestry than it is about religion.[5]

As far as Christians are concerned, the number of self-identified Christians in America has been shrinking. Ninety percent in the early 1970s, it is now only about two-thirds of all adults. Some 29 percent of all Americans now claim to have no religious affiliation. But although there are fewer self-identified Christians overall, those who are radicalized are far better organized and far more vocal and politically active than in the past. Many do not accept the separation of church and state at all and support the establishment of Christianity as the national religion.[6]

Evidence of their political tenacity and clout can be seen in a sampling of recent state-level initiatives regarding the public schools. In 2023, Texas lawmakers approved legislation to allow unlicensed religious chaplains to replace guidance counselors in the state's public schools, rejecting an amendment that would have barred them from attempting to convert students. The governor of Mississippi signed a measure to permit students to pray at school events, over school intercoms, and before school athletic contests. An Arkansas school district permitted faculty to distribute copies of the New Testament to fifth and sixth graders and allowed them to lead prekindergartners in prayer. And Oklahoma officials approved plans for a taxpayer-funded Catholic charter school.[7]

That such measures have sometimes succeeded is evidence that the legal environment, too, has changed. The liberal-minded Warren Court that gave us *Engel v. Vitale* is ancient history, and what we have today—thanks in large part to the assiduous efforts of the Christian right—is a right-leaning court bent on limiting the power of the federal government and hostile to church-state separation. Witness the court's 2022 departures from precedent in which it required the state of Maine to fund religious education at parochial schools as part of a tuition assistance program in one decision, and in another permitted a public high school coach to kneel and pray with his players on the football field in what it deemed "personal religious observance."[8]

Christian nationalists are counting on this shift to the right as they attempt to revisit issues regarding school prayer, the teaching of creationism, school vouchers, and released time, some of which were ostensibly settled decades ago. Legislation recently adopted in Louisiana to require that the Ten Commandments be displayed in every public school classroom, for example, is patently illegal under the 1980 Supreme Court decision in *Stone v. Graham*, in which the court overturned a similar law in Kentucky because it had "no secular legislative purpose" and was "plainly religious in nature." But proponents of the measure are hoping that the Roberts Court, which has already shown its willingness to disregard direct precedent, might opt to reverse the earlier decision.[9]

As far as the Christmas holiday itself is concerned, it seems to have lost much of its religious character. A recent survey found that most American adults find the religious features of the holiday far less important now than in the past, and that the percentage who believe in the divine aspects of the Christmas story—the babe in the manger, born to a virgin—has shrunk. Add to that the fact that the holiday is often diluted by being lumped together with Hanukkah and Kwanzaa in "holiday season" celebrations, the crass commercialism associated with the season, and the ubiquity of carols in the media, and it is probably fair to say that for many, Christmas is now far more about tinsel and presents than it is about the birth of a savior.[10]

The Christian right has been adept at setting plenty of fires for the ADL, the American Jewish Congress, and the American Jewish Committee, Lucas's most likely Jewish heirs in the battle over Christmas in the schools, to put out. The Jewish organizations have focused their legal efforts on submitting amicus briefs in such cases, including *Engel v. Vitale*, *Abington Township v. Schempp*, and, more recently, *Kennedy v. Bremerton School District*. Other organizations, like the ACLU, the Americans United for Separation of Church and State, and the Freedom from Religion Foundation, are more visible in filing suits against school systems that violate the Establishment Clause, which, after all, has never been, nor should be, exclusively a Jewish concern.

For their part, the Jewish groups now mostly content themselves with public education and with opining on what they believe is allowed, may or may not be allowed, and is not allowed in the way of school Christmas celebrations. None appears to have any appetite for pressing the issue further, that is, for a full-frontal assault aimed at banishing the holiday, and *all* religious holidays for that matter, from the classroom. Even though the Supreme Court has never explicitly ruled on Christmas celebrations in the schools, these groups have surely read the handwriting on the wall and probably accepted the inevitability of such celebrations. Today they seek primarily to limit the school celebrations' more grossly sectarian aspects.

Many, of course, still believe there is nothing that can ever be done to make a holiday that marks the birth of a Christian savior truly secular, and that the law, properly interpreted, simply does not permit such celebrations in the schools. But that conviction appears to be trumped by the realization that to continue to pursue the matter will almost certainly be fruitless. Given the politicization of the current Supreme Court, its readiness to assault traditional notions of church-state separation, and its willingness to reverse precedents and inject religion even further into the public square—witness Justice Samuel A. Alito's widely quoted remark about the need for the United States to return "to a place of godliness"—the chances of a sweeping ruling remanding Christmas celebrations to churches, parochial schools, and homes seem unlikely.[11]

The Jewish advocacy groups no doubt realize that a continued push would likely spur more backlash than any serious change in policy—a lesson Albert Lucas learned the hard way more than a century earlier. Put another way, the leveling of the bogus charge of a Jewish "war on Christmas" is surely as inevitable today as it was in 1906, if not more so. There is already a very public spat about the use of the more inclusive expression "Happy Holidays" in place of "Merry Christmas"; Donald Trump stoked the coals of this silly, made-up dispute during his first term in the White House, and the Texas legislature actually passed a law in 2013 expressly permitting the Christmas greeting in the public schools. In the twenty-first century, there may well be a better chance of opposition morphing into violence against Jews, especially given the emergence and legitimization of the radical white Christian nationalist movement, the huge rise in antisemitism in the wake of the Israel-Hamas war, and the ability of social media to inflame passions and help extremists identify one another and coordinate their efforts.[12]

Although the *exact* phrase "separation of church and state" does not appear in the Constitution—something Christian nationalists like to point out—the framers' intent in this regard is quite clear. The First Amendment, which bars laws "respecting an establishment of religion or prohibiting the free exercise thereof," taken together with the overall secular nature of the document (which, by the way, also includes no mention of Christianity) and the explicit proscription against religious tests for public office holders, enshrine the concept of church-state separation.

That is why in our age, when, according to the Pew Research Center, fully 45 percent of Americans more or less agree that America is or should be a Christian nation and an appalling six out of ten believe the founders *intended* this, there is a stronger than ever case to be made for the bright red line Albert Lucas sought to keep officially sanctioned devotional prayer, religious celebrations, proselytizing, and sectarianism out of the schools.[13]

Such a line would ensure that the rights of minorities like Jews, Muslims, atheists, agnostics, polytheists, and others are not trampled, as they too often are today. But today's Congress is not a body apt to draw such a line, nor would the current Supreme Court be likely to uphold it. Jews, therefore, are ostensibly in more or less in the same position in which the New York Board of Education left them in 1907: forced to accept celebrations of a holiday in which they do not believe in the public schools attended by their children, paid for in part by their tax dollars.[14]

In an ironic way, however, time has accomplished what Albert Lucas could not. Christmas pageants have not been eliminated, to be sure, but they are fewer in number, and far less religious in heavily Jewish school systems if they are held at all. Time has produced a far more assimilated Jewish population and a far less sectarian holiday.

If Lucas were alive today, he would surely take cold comfort in this state of affairs. He would no doubt be alarmed at the lack of orthodoxy among the vast majority of America's Jews, which he would have good reason to view as a triumph of the forces against which he struggled so assiduously. But in a very narrow sense he could declare victory, as Christmas celebrations no longer pose the existential threat to Jewish school children that he was certain they did in 1906.

Chronology

1805

A Free School Society is established in New York City to provide a basic education for children whose families are not affiliated with any religious denomination.

1807

The Free School Society begins to receive funding from the New York state legislature.

1822

Baptists ask the legislature for public money for their church schools and are put on a similar footing with the Free School Society.

1824

Lobbied by the Free School Society, the legislature delegates the right to choose local grantees to the Common Council of the City of New York, which cuts all state funding to church schools the following year.

1840

In a sop to Catholics, New York governor William H. Seward proposes that immigrant children be educated in state-funded schools by others of the same faith. Bishop John Hughes unsuccessfully presses the Common Council for public support for Catholic schools.

1842

The New York state legislature places public education in the hands of locally elected ward commissioners but bans sectarian teaching in the state's public schools.

1844

The legislature amends the law to deny the New York City Board of Education the power to exclude the Bible from its public schools. That same year, the board rules that the reading of the Bible, as long as it is not accompanied by note or comment, does not constitute sectarianism.

1849

The legislature requires school districts throughout the state to offer a free common school education, funded by tax revenues, to all children.

1852

Reform rabbi Isaac Mayer Wise, then chaplain of the New York state legislature, attacks sectarianism in the schools.

1898

The five boroughs are consolidated into the City of Greater New York, whose new charter prohibits schools receiving public money from teaching sectarian doctrines.

Rabbi Henry Pereira Mendes invites fifty congregations to establish the Union of Orthodox Jewish Congregations of America and Canada (also known as the Orthodox Union) and Albert Lucas is chosen as a secretary of the new organization. Its chief goals are to defend traditional Judaism against all threats and to oppose the Reform movement.

1900

Lucas launches a program of instruction in Jewish learning for youth that eventually embraces several local synagogues. It continues for many years and educates thousands of Jewish children.

He also writes principals of several Lower East Side schools protesting reading from the New Testament and compelling Jewish students to attend school on the Jewish High Holy Days.

1903

June

Lucas delivers a paper at the third annual convention of the Orthodox Union decrying Christian missions on the East Side that surreptitiously seek converts from among Jewish children.

Lucas, Mendes, and Rabbi Bernard Drachman meet New York City Superintendent of Schools William Henry Maxwell to protest Christianity in the public schools.

August

Lucas roundly criticizes the highly respected photojournalist and social reformer Jacob A. Riis for his mission's proselytizing among Jews.

November 10

Superintendent Maxwell issues a circular directing district superintendents to "instruct principals that hymns containing reference to the tenets of any religious sect are out of place in unsectarian schools and should not be used."

1904

September 19

P.S. 144, an elementary school in Brownsville, Brooklyn, opens its doors with Frank Fountain Harding as its first principal.

1905

December

Attorney Edward Herbert, a P.S. 144 parent, writes Principal Harding to warn him against injecting religion into school activities and decorating classrooms with icons "offensive to the Jewish faith."

December 19

In an assembly, Harding exhorts students, most of whom are Jewish, to "be like Christ." He is challenged by fourteen-year-old Augusta Herbert, Edward Herbert's daughter.

December 21

A petition to the District 39 School Committee circulates in Brownsville, accusing Harding of establishing a policy to "systematically Christianize children born and raised in the Jewish faith" and seeking his dismissal by the board of education.

1906

January 17

The District 39 School Committee, chaired by Austrian-born Jew Baruch Miller, holds the first of two hearings on the Harding case. The Orthodox Union sends attorneys to "prosecute" the case. Although the charge of "systematically Christianizing" Jewish students is dropped, Harding is accused of reading from the New Testament, leading sectarian songs and prayers, allowing the display of sectarian images, and commenting on the Scriptures.

January 30

The second and final hearing on the Harding case is held. Attorneys are permitted two weeks to submit briefs on the legal issues before a decision is rendered.

January 31

The *Brooklyn Daily Eagle* prints a petition with sixteen hundred signatories commending Harding and protesting the allegations against him. Other newspapers run letters to the editor critical of the case.

March 26

The District 39 School Committee dismisses all charges against Principal Harding, garnering a furious reaction from the local Yiddish press. The case is referred to the full board of education.

May 29

The board of education's Committee on Elementary Education holds a hearing to review the Harding case. Chaired by German-Jewish attorney Abraham Stern, it hears testimony from the Orthodox Union leadership and several Orthodox and Reform rabbis. Harding declines to appear.

June 13

The Committee on Elementary Education reports to the full board of education its decision "not to interfere with the conclusions of the local board" but, finding Harding's conduct "indiscreet," recommends that the board not "fully exonerate" Harding. The board records its disapproval of his actions.

June 21

Physicians engaged by the board of health visit P.S. 110 and remove the adenoids from some eighty-one ostensibly "defective" children, giving rise to false rumors that some children have died from the procedure.

June 27–28

When it is discovered that doctors are once again visiting the schools of the Lower East Side, frantic Jewish parents, believing their children's throats are being cut, descend on a dozen elementary schools. The following day, something similar happens in Brooklyn.

July

The Central Conference of American Rabbis, the rabbinic leadership organization of the Reform movement, publishes a pamphlet entitled *Why the Bible Should Not Be Read in the Public Schools* to counter what it sees as a calculated effort by Christian organizations to insinuate Bible reading into the schools.

December 11

At a hearing in advance of the Christmas holiday convened at the request of Albert Lucas, rabbis of all stripes petition the Committee on Elementary Schools to issue an order prohibiting Christmas observances in the public schools. The committee pledges to bring the matter to the full board on December 19 but fails to do so.

December 23

In the absence of board action, it becomes clear that Christmas 1906 will be business as usual in the public schools. Appeals appear in two Yiddish newspapers to all Jewish parents to keep their children home the next day, December 24, when schools are slated to hold their Christmas celebrations.

December 24

As many as a third of all Jewish children are absent from school; in some schools the figure is as high as seventy-five percent. But some of the schools boycotted had not planned to hold Christmas celebrations in the first place. Reaction in the press is mixed.

1907

January 9

Committee on Elementary Education chairman Abraham Stern finally submits to the full board of education his committee's recommendations for system-wide standards to govern Christmas celebrations in the public schools. The document suggests forbidding the singing of sectarian hymns, the reading of religious treatises other than the Bible, and the assignment of essays on religious topics. It does not ban Christmas exercises, but does urge that care be taken to eliminate sectarian material from them.

January 13

Twenty-five Jewish girls who refused to take part in Christmas exercises at P.S. 141 in east Williamsburg are notified that they will not be permitted to participate in commencement exercises later in the month. The girls decide to hold a ceremony in a private venue.

February 13

The board of education approves the recommendations of the Stern committee with one amendment. Without explanation, it drops the phrase "song books containing songs and hymns of this character [i.e., sectarian] should be stricken from the list of textbooks."

May 21

The board of education's Committee on Text-Books and Supplies directs the Committee on Supplies to instruct the publishers of books sold to the school system to eliminate sectarian hymns if they wish to continue to do business with the system.

The Committee on Supplies, in turn, bucks the matter to the Committee on Studies and Text-Books, whose chairman refuses to issue the order. The publishers get the message anyway.

June

Principal Frank Fountain Harding is transferred to P.S. 11 in Brooklyn's Clinton Hill neighborhood, a community in which few Jews live.

November 20

The music director of the New York public schools warns principals to avoid carols in upcoming Christmas celebrations in which Christ or Christmas is mentioned. The admonition is reported in the *New York Times* the following day and sets off a firestorm of protest.

November 24–26

Dozens of indignant letters are printed in local and far-flung newspapers accusing the board of education of what one called "anti-sectarianism gone mad." Many are antisemitic. Many Christian pastors also resort to inflammatory rhetoric. Massive pressure is visited on the board.

November 27

The board adopts a disingenuous motion to clarify that it "did not intend by the passage of said resolutions to abolish Christmas exercises as heretofore conducted in the public schools," and that it had not "directed changes in any books or in any songs." Despite this, hate-filled letters to the editor continue for several more days.

December 6

Lucas calls for a second boycott, but there is no appetite for this among major Jewish groups.

1947

December

Isaac Bildersee, the Jewish assistant superintendent of schools in charge of two districts in Brooklyn, declares that carols with reference to the Nativity may not be sung in upcoming school Christmas exercises. The predictable storm of protest from Christian groups follows. Although he nominally receives support from his superiors, he is in fact undermined by them, and his order is essentially rescinded.

1951

The New York State Board of Regents, which regulates education in the state, proposes a nondenominational prayer that might be adopted by local boards and recited in the public schools voluntarily by children of all stripes. Reaction is mixed and acceptance is slow.

1956

The American Jewish Committee distributes a memorandum, "Dealing with the Christmas Observance in the Public Schools," that warns of the dangers of local Jewish communities objecting to Christmas pageants. It is a far cry from the approach of Albert Lucas a half century earlier.

1958

Nine residents of New Hyde Park, New York, including Steven Engel, a Jew, object to the Regents' Prayer and sue the local school board—and its president,

William Vitale—on the grounds that school prayer of any kind is unconstitutional. The case of *Engel v. Vitale* proceeds through the judicial system.

1962

The U.S. Supreme Court under Chief Justice Earl Warren rules in the case of *Engel v. Vitale* that state-sanctioned prayer in public schools, voluntary or not, violates the Establishment Clause of the First Amendment to the Constitution.

1963

In the case of *Abington Township v. Schempp*, the Supreme Court finds Bible reading in schools in Pennsylvania and Maryland unconstitutional as well. Its decision invalidates Bible reading and recitation of the Lord's Prayer in the nation's public schools. Efforts in Congress to reverse these rulings are unsuccessful.

1971

In deciding the Pennsylvania case of *Lemon v. Kurtzman*, the U.S. Supreme Court devises a three-pronged test to decide whether a state statute violates the Constitution's Establishment Clause. Known as the "Lemon Test," it is employed for nearly forty years before being jettisoned in 2022.

2021

The Anti-Defamation League publishes principles designed to "help" school administrators and teachers plan their holiday celebrations with its interpretation of what is and is not allowed. Neither the ADL nor any of the major Jewish groups appears to favor continuing to pursue the elimination of Christmas exercises from the public schools, probably for fear of antisemitic backlash and low expectations of any legal relief, especially from the right-leaning Supreme Court and the Congress.

2022

The Roberts Supreme Court abandons the 1971 "Lemon Test" to determine whether a law violates the First Amendment's Establishment Clause and, in the case of *Kennedy v. Bremerton School District*, holds that a public school employee leading students in prayer during public school sports activities is protected speech.

Further Reading

ON ALBERT LUCAS AND THE ORTHODOX UNION

Gurock, Jeffrey S. "Why Albert Lucas Did Not Serve in the New York Kehillah." *Proceedings of the American Academy for Jewish Research* 51 (1984): 55–72.

Medoff, Rafael. "The Orthodox Union's Early Years: Fighting for Jewish Rights in a Very Different America." *Jewish Action* (Spring 2016).

ON RABBI HENRY PEREIRA MENDES

Markovitz, Eugene. "Henry Pereira Mendes: Architect of the Union of Orthodox Jewish Congregations of America." *American Jewish Historical Quarterly* 55, no. 3 (March 1966): 364–65, 367–84.

ON THE 1906 SCHOOL BOYCOTT

Bloom, Leonard. "A Successful Jewish Boycott of the New York City Public Schools—Christmas 1906." *American Jewish History* 70, no. 2 (December 1980): 180–88.

Manseau, Peter. "The Great Christmas Strike of 1906." *New York Times*, December 29, 2015.

ON JACOB A. RIIS AND THE SETTLEMENT MOVEMENT

Berman, Myron. "A New Spirit on the East Side: The Early History of the Emanu-El Brotherhood." *American Jewish History* 54, no. 1 (September 1, 1964): 53–81.

Gurock, Jeffrey S. "Jacob A. Riis: Christian Friend or Missionary Foe? Two Jewish Views." *American Jewish History* 71, no. 1 (September 1981): 29–47.

Riis, Jacob A. *How the Other Half Lives: Studies among the Tenements of New York*. Mineola NY: Dover Publications, 1971.

ON THE LOWER EAST SIDE JEWISH COMMUNITY

Hindus, Milton, ed. *The Jewish East Side, 1881–1924*. New Brunswick NJ: Transaction Publishers, 1996.

Howe, Irving, *World of Our Fathers: The Journey of the East European Jews to America and the Life They Found and Made*. New York: Schocken Books, 1990.

Polland, Annie, and Daniel Soyer. *Emerging Metropolis: New York Jews in the Age of Immigration, 1840–1920*. New York: New York University Press, 2012.

Richin, Moses. *The Promised City: New York's Jews, 1870–1914*. Cambridge MA: Harvard University Press, 1962.

Sarna, Jonathan D. *American Judaism: A History*. New Haven CT: Yale University Press, 2004.

Seligman, Scott D. *The Great Kosher Meat War of 1902: Immigrant Housewives and the Riots That Shook New York City*. Lincoln NE: Potomac Books, 2020.

Weinberger, Moses. *People Walk on Their Heads: Jews and Judaism in New York*. Translated by Jonathan D. Sarna. New York: Holmes and Meyer Publishers, 1982.

ON JEWS IN THE PUBLIC SCHOOLS

Cohen, Naomi W. *Jews in Christian America: The Pursuit of Religious Equality*. Oxford: Oxford University Press, 1992.

Rumberg, Stephan F. *Going to America, Going to School: The Jewish Immigrant Public School Encounter in Turn-of-the-Century New York City*. New York: Praeger, 1986.

Sarna, Jonathan D., and David G. Dalin. *Religion and State in the American Jewish Experience*. Notre Dame IN: University of Notre Dame Press, 1997.

ON THE ADENOIDS RIOT

Ribak, Gil. "'They Are Slitting the Throats of Jewish Children': The 1906 New York School Riots and Contending Images of Gentiles." *American Jewish History* 94, no. 3 (September 2008): 175–96.

Portnoy, Eddy. "Sore." *Tablet*, August 19, 2010, www.tabletmag.com/sections/community/articles/sore.

ON THE HISTORY OF THE NEW YORK PUBLIC SCHOOL SYSTEM

Bourne, Wm. Oakland. *History of the Public School Society of the City of New York*. New York: Wm. Wood, 1870.

Palmer, A. Emerson. *The New York Public School: Being a History of Free Education in the City of New York*. New York: Macmillan, 1905.

Randall, S. S. *History of the Common School System of the State of New York*. New York: Ivison, Blakeman, Taylor, 1871.

ON THE NEW YORK KEHILLAH

Goren, Arthur A. *New York Jews and the Quest for Community: The Kehillah Experiment, 1908–1922*. New York: Columbia University Press, 1970.

Notes

PROLOGUE

1. "Sunshine Society Plans Many Christmas Trees," *Brooklyn Citizen*, December 10, 1905; Chapman and Company advertisement, *Brooklyn Citizen*, December 10, 1905; The Berlin advertisement, *Brooklyn Citizen*, December 10, 1905; Rev. Dr. J. F. Carson, "The Coming of the King: God's Christmas Message," *Brooklyn Citizen*, December 10, 1905.
2. Department of Education, City of New York, *Fourth Annual Report of the City Superintendent of Schools to the Board of Education of the City of New York for the Year Ending July 31, 1902* (New York: Department of Education, 1902), 22; "First School Baths Opened," *Brooklyn Times Union*, July 24, 1905.
3. New York Department of Finance, *Reports of an Investigation Concerning the Cost of Maintaining the Public School System of the City of New York: Together with Analysis of the Board of Education Departmental Estimate for 1906* (New York: M. B. Brown, 1905), 64; "Great Crush at Brooklyn Schools," *Brooklyn Standard Union*, September 12, 1904; "New Schools Are Needed, but Money Is Lacking," *Brooklyn Daily Eagle*, January 8, 1906; "Back to School the Children Rush Today," *Brooklyn Standard Union*, September 11, 1905.
4. Department of Education, City of New York, *Fourth Annual Report of the City Superintendent of Schools to the Board of Education of the City of New York for the Year Ending July 31, 1902* (New York: Department of Education, 1902), 18; Department of Education, City of New York, *Fourth Annual Report of the City Superintendent of Schools to the Board of Education of the City of New York for the Year Ending July 31, 1902* (New York: Department of Education, 1902), 21; "News of the Schools," *Globe and Commercial Advertiser*, May 25, 1904.
5. "General School News," *Brooklyn Daily Eagle*, October 17, 1895; "General School News," *Brooklyn Daily Eagle*, December 15, 1895; "Brooklyn School News," *Brooklyn Daily Eagle*, March 9, 1896; "William Augustus Harding," *Brooklyn Daily Eagle*, July 9, 1898.

6. "Public School Pupils Begin Weeks' Vacation," *Brooklyn Daily Eagle*, December 22, 1905; Paul Ritterband, *Counting the Jews of New York, 1900–1991: An Essay in Substance and Method*, 222, Institute of Contemporary Jewry, Policy Commons, accessed March 16, 2023, policycommons.net/artifacts/1171724/counting-the-jews-in-new-york-1900-1991/1724852; "Brownsville News," *Brooklyn Citizen*, December 19, 1905.
7. William J. Shearer, *Gems of Wisdom from Bible Literature and Proverbs* (New York: Richard, Smith, 1904), 7–8, 84. The exact citation is Acts 13:45.
8. "Told Jewish Pupils of Christ," *New York Post*, March 10, 1906; "Our Children's Rights Must Be Safeguarded," *Hebrew Standard*, November 29, 1907.
9. "Christmas Celebrations in the Public Schools," *Hebrew Standard*, December 29, 1905; "Brownsville Demands Harding's Dismissal," *Brooklyn Citizen*, December 22, 1905.
10. "Brownsville Wants School Principal Harding Removed," *Brooklyn Standard Union*, December 22, 1905.

1. THIS UNION OF CHURCH AND STATE

1. Untitled, *Morning Chronicle* (New York), November 29, 1805; Arthur Jackson Hall, *Religious Education in the Public Schools of the State and City of New York: A Historical Study* (Chicago: University of Chicago Press, 1914), 21–22; A. Emerson Palmer, *The New York Public School: Being a History of Free Education in the City of New York* (New York: Macmillan, 1905), xxiv–xxv.
2. S. S. Randall, *History of the Common School System in the State of New York* (New York: Ivison, Blakeman, Taylor, 1871), 102.
3. John W. Pratt, "Conflict in the Development of the New York City Public School System," *History of Education Quarterly* 5, no. 2 (June 1965), 110–20.
4. James W. Fraser, *The School in the United States: A Documentary History* (Boston: McGraw Hill, 2001), 74–80.
5. "Common Council," *Truth Teller*, October 31, 1840; "Board of Aldermen," *New York Commercial Advertiser*, November 17, 1840; "Bishop Hughes' Reply," *Albany Argus*, December 10, 1841.
6. "Common School Fund," *New York Commercial Advertiser*, December 3, 1840.
7. John W. Pratt, "Conflict in the Development of the New York City Public School System," *History of Education Quarterly* 5, no. 2 (June 1965), 110–20; "Triumph of the Roman Catholics," *Democratic Journal*, April 27, 1842; Ian Bartrum, "The Political Origins of Secular Public Education: The New York School Controversy, 1840–1842," *NYU Journal of Law and Liberty* 3, no. 2 (2008), 268–87.
8. Diane Ravitch, *The Great School Wars: New York City, 1805–1973* (New York: Basic Books, 1974), 80.
9. Arthur Jackson Hall, *Religious Education in the Public Schools of the State and City of New York: A Historical Study* (Chicago: University of Chicago Press, 1914), 78–84; Ravitch, *Great School Wars*, 80.
10. Editorial, *New York Tribune*, March 8, 1842; S. S. Randall, *History of the Common School System in the State of New York* (New York: Ivison, Blakeman, Taylor, 1871), 195–96.

11. "Congregational Schools," *Asmonean*, October 22, 1852; Max B. May, *Isaac Mayer Wise: The Founder of American Judaism* (New York: G. P. Putnam's Sons, 1916), 133.
12. *Report of the Select Committee of the Board of Education to Which Was Referred a Communication from the Trustees of the Fourth Ward, in Relation to the Sectarian Character of Certain Books in Use in the Schools of That Ward* (New York: Levi D. Slamm, 1843), 5–8; Hyman B. Grinstein, *The Rise of the Jewish Community of New York, 1654–1860* (Philadelphia: Jewish Publication Society of America, 1945), 235–37.
13. "Answers to Frequently Asked Questions about Blaine Amendments," Institute for Justice, accessed September 6, 2023, ij.org/issues/school-choice/blaine-amendments/answers-frequently-asked-questions-blaine-amendments/.
14. "Manufacturing Citizens," *New York Tribune*, September 7, 1907.
15. Richard Ariel Weiss, "The Children of the Concrete: Jewish Immigrants in the New York Public School System at the Turn of the 20th Century" (master's thesis, Concordia University, Montreal, Quebec, 1997), 20–21.
16. "The Facts in the Case," *American Hebrew*, November 15, 1889.
17. The Greater New York Charter, as enacted in 1897, sec. 1151, Hathitrust, accessed February 25, 2025, catalog.hathitrust.org/Record/009037976.
18. "Christianity in Public Schools," *Hebrew Standard*, February 22, 1907.

2. COLLECTORS OF STRAY LAMBS

1. "Register of Pupils at the City of London School 1861–1879," City of London School Digital Archive, accessed July 30, 2024, www.clsarchive.org.uk/MEDIA/Registers/pdf/CLSReg1861_79.pdf; Rev. Jacob Goldstein, "A Stalwart Fighter," *Hebrew Standard*, January 8, 1909; U.S., Passport Applications, 1795–1925, Ancestry, accessed February 25, 2025, www.ancestry.com/search/collections/1174/records/1584388; 1871 England Census, Ancestry, accessed February 25, 2025, https://www.ancestry.com/discoveryui-content/view/2344574:7619.
2. Goldstein, "Stalwart Fighter."
3. "Married," *Hebrew Standard*, September 14, 1900; "Lucas-Nieto," *New York World*, December 25, 1890; "Rev. A. H. Nieto Dies at 82," *Denver Jewish News*, August 27, 1919.
4. Goldstein, "Stalwart Fighter."
5. "The Kindergarten at Centre No. 2," *Hebrew Standard*, September 28, 1906.
6. "Heroic Measures Needed," *American Hebrew*, January 8, 1897.
7. Rafael Medoff, "The Orthodox Union's Early Years: Fighting for Jewish Rights in a Very Different America," Jewish Action, accessed January 8, 2023, jewishaction.com/jewish-world/history/the-orthodox-unions-early-years-fighting-for-jewish-rights-in-a-very-different-america/; "The Orthodox Conference," *The Jewish South*, March 4, 1898.
8. "Orthodox Jews in Convention," *San Francisco Call*, December 31, 1900; "Communications: The Sunday Service," *American Hebrew*, December 1, 1899; "Not to Wed Gentiles," *St. Paul Globe*, December 31, 1900; "New York Jews and Judaism," *American Israelite*, April 18, 1901; "Of Interest to Jewish Students," *Hebrew Standard*, July 24, 1903; "Hebrew Holidays at Home" *New York Sun*, September 14, 1898.

9. Frank Moss, *The American Metropolis from Knickerbocker Days to the Present Time* (New York: Authors' Syndicate, 1897), vol. 3, 159; "The Book of the Week," *New York Herald*, January 23, 1898.
10. "Frank Moss and His Book," *Hebrew Standard*, August 9, 1901.
11. "Opposed to the New Rabbi," *New York Sun*, August 12, 1888; Eugene Markovitz, "Henry Pereira Mendes: Architect of the Union of Orthodox Jewish Congregations of America," *American Jewish Historical Quarterly* 55, no. 3 (March 1966): 368, quoting Morris Weinberger, *Ha-Yehudim veha-Yahadut be-New York* (New York: n.p., 1887), 22.
12. Albert Lucas, "Religion in Education," *Hebrew Standard*, June 26, 1903.
13. "Albert Lucas," *New York Times*, June 18, 1923; "Honor Mr. Lucas for Good Work for His Faith," *New York World*, December 30, 1908; Jeffrey S. Gurock, "Why Albert Lucas Did Not Serve in the New York Kehillah," *Proceedings of the American Academy for Jewish Research* 51 (1984): 56; "General Items of the Week," *New York Tribune*, April 8, 1905.
14. Lucas, "Religion in Education."
15. "A Voice from the Ghetto," *American Hebrew*, August 14, 1903.
16. Jacob Riis, "The Jews of New York," *Review of Reviews*, January 1896; Jacob A. Riis, *How the Other Half Lives* (New York: Charles Scribner's Sons, 1932), 112.
17. "A Voice from the Ghetto."
18. "A Voice from the Ghetto."
19. "Work of the Riis Settlement," *New York Post*, September 16, 1903.
20. "Work of the Riis Settlement."
21. Jeffrey S. Gurock, "Jacob A. Riis: Christian Friend or Missionary Foe? Two Jewish Views," *American Jewish History* 71, 1 (September 1981): 32–34.

3. GIVE UP CHRISTMAS TRADITIONS

1. "Union of Orthodox Congregations of the United States and Canada," *Hebrew Standard*, June 12, 1903.
2. Albert Lucas, "Religion in Education," *Hebrew Standard*, June 26, 1903.
3. "Waste in School Funds," *New York Tribune*, February 5, 1905; Albert Lucas, "Religion in Education," *Hebrew Standard*, June 26, 1903.
4. "Correspondence," *Hebrew Standard*, February 28, 1908.
5. Lucas, "Religion in Education"; "Orthodox Hebrews Meet," *New York Sun*, June 22, 1903; "Raps King's Daughters," *New York Tribune*, June 22, 1903; Albert Lucas, "The Harding Case," *American Hebrew and Jewish Messenger*, April 13, 1906; "Christianity in Public Schools," *Hebrew Standard*, February 22, 1907.
6. "Roman Catholic Bibles in the Public Schools," *Brooklyn Standard Union*, November 19, 1903; "The Douay Bible in the Public Schools," *New York Tribune*, April 5, 1903; "The Bible in the Public Schools," *New York Sun*, March 1, 1903.
7. "Christian Hymns in Public Schools," *American Hebrew and Jewish Messenger*, December 25, 1903.
8. "Message of Rabbi Jos. Krauskopf, President of the Central Conference of American Rabbis, to the Fifteenth Annual Convention, Louisville KY, June 27, 1904," *Jewish Voice*, July 8, 1904.

9. Max Heller, "A Compromise," *American Israelite*, June 9, 1904.
10. "Three New Studies Added," *Plain Dealer* (Cleveland OH), September 24, 1901; "Contrary to Justice," *Plain Dealer*, September 27, 1901; "Brave Men Turn to Be Cowards," *Plain Dealer*, October 7, 1901; "Religion in Public Schools," *Jewish Comment*, October 11, 1901; "Every Member Was Visited," *Plain Dealer*, September 27, 1901; "Against Religion in Schools," *Plain Dealer*, September 26, 1901.
11. "Christmas Carols," *Deseret Evening News*, December 18, 1901; "Christmas Carols in Public Schools," *Hebrew Standard*, December 27, 1901.
12. "St. Joseph, Mo.," *Jewish Voice*, October 23, 1903; "Scriptures Are Banished from Schools," *San Francisco Call*, April 8, 1903.
13. "The Outlook," *Christian Statesman*, 40, no. 5 (May 1906): 133–34.
14. "Christmas Carols Cut Out," *New York Sun*, December 24, 1905; "Christmas Carols Cut Out," *Daily Morning Journal and Courier*, December 25, 1905; "Christmas Carol Question," *Daily Morning Journal and Courier*, December 27, 1905; "Prohibits Carols at New Haven," *Boston Herald*, December 24, 1905; "Jottings," *American Hebrew and Jewish Messenger*, January 4, 1906.

4. AN UNFIT MAN

1. "Brownsville Wants School Principal Harding Removed," *Brooklyn Standard Union*, December 22, 1905.
2. "Brownsville News," *Brooklyn Citizen*, January 10, 1906.
3. "Brownsville Demands Harding's Dismissal," *Brooklyn Citizen*, December 22, 1905.
4. Advertisement, *Forverts*, December 14, 1903; "Excitement at Trial of Principal Harding," *Brooklyn Daily Eagle*, January 18, 1906; Edward Herbert, "An Unknown Celebrity," *Hebrew Standard*, October 26, 1917.
5. "Brownsville Demands Harding's Dismissal."
6. "The New School System," *New York Tribune*, November 9, 1901.
7. "Christmas Celebrations in the Public Schools," *Hebrew Standard*, December 29, 1905; "Excitement at Trial of Principal Harding," *Brooklyn Daily Eagle*, January 18, 1906.
8. "Brownsville Wants School Principal Harding Removed."
9. "Public Schools Begin Week's Vacation," *Brooklyn Daily Eagle*, December 22, 1905.
10. "A Jewish Edict," *Evening Times-Republican* (Marshalltown IA), December 23, 1904.
11. Albert Lucas, "Christmas in Our Public Schools," *Hebrew Standard*, December 15, 1905; Albert Lucas, "Public School Religion," *American Hebrew and Jewish Messenger*, December 15, 1905.
12. "Christmas Taught School Children," *Frank Leslie's Weekly*, December 9, 1905.
13. "Christmas in Public Schools," *American Hebrew and Jewish Messenger*, December 29, 1905; Selma C. Berrol, "William Henry Maxwell and a New Educational New York," *History of Education Quarterly* 8, no. 2 (Summer, 1968): 215–28.
14. "Public School Cooking," *New York Tribune*, April 8, 1900.
15. "Brownsville News," *Brooklyn Citizen*, January 10, 1906.
16. "Christian Teaching in the Public Schools," *Hebrew Standard*, December 29, 1905.

5. SYSTEMATICALLY CHRISTIANIZING

1. "Baruch Miller," *New York Times*, October 4, 1927; "84's Alumni Association," *Brooklyn Daily Eagle*, November 22, 1907; 1900 United States Federal Census, Ancestry, accessed February 25, 2025, www.ancestry.com/search/collections/7602/records/55670338; 1910 United States Federal Census, Ancestry, accessed February 25, 2025, www.ancestry.com/search/collections/7884/records/17994978.
2. "Baruch Miller"; "84's Alumni Association"; "Judaic Critics Attack Principal of No. 144," *Brooklyn Daily Eagle*, January 13, 1906; "News of Brownsville," *Brooklyn Citizen*, January 13, 1906.
3. "Jews Turn on Schoolmaster," *New York Sun*, January 14, 1906.
4. "Local News," *American Hebrew and Jewish Messenger*, January 5, 1906; "Brownsville News," *Brooklyn Citizen*, January 10, 1906; "Judaic Critics Attack Principal of No. 144"; "Interesting Items," *Jewish Voice*, January 26, 1906.
5. "Plan to Improve the Poor," *New York Tribune*, December 10, 1899; "To Improve Brownsville," *New York Tribune*, November 26, 1900.
6. "Trial of Frank F. Harding, School Principal, Begins," *Brooklyn Citizen*, January 18, 1906.
7. "Local News," *American Hebrew and Jewish Messenger*, January 19, 1906; "Trial of Frank F. Harding, School Principal, Begins"; "The Trial," *Die Wahrheit*, January 18, 1906.
8. "The Action against Principal Harding," *Hebrew Standard*, January 26, 1906.
9. *Greater New York Charter as Enacted in 1897*, section 1098 (Albany NY: Weed-Parsons Printing, 1897), 552.
10. "Excitement at Trial of Principal Harding," *Brooklyn Daily Eagle*, January 18, 1906.
11. "Excitement at Trial of Principal Harding."
12. "Trial of Frank F. Harding, School Principal, Begins," *Brooklyn Citizen*, January 18, 1906.
13. "Principal Is Commended," *Brooklyn Daily Eagle*, January 31, 1906.
14. Scott D. Seligman, *The Great Kosher Meat War of 1902: Immigrant Housewives and the Riots That Shook New York City* (Lincoln NE: Potomac Books, 2020).
15. "The Antisemites of Brownsville," *Die Wahrheit*, March 14, 1906.
16. "Shapiro's Anger," *Die Wahrheit*, January 25, 1906.
17. "Religion in the Schools," *Brooklyn Daily Eagle*, January 22, 1906.

6. I WILL SPEAK ABOUT CHRIST

1. "Charge against Principal Harding," *Hebrew Standard*, February 2, 1906.
2. "Charge against Principal Harding."
3. "Laughter and Applause at Principal's Trial," *Brooklyn Daily Eagle*, January 31, 1906; "Hearing of Harding Ends: School Board to Decide," *Brooklyn Citizen*, January 31, 1906; "Principal Makes a Denial of Charge," *Brooklyn Times*, January 31, 1906.
4. "A Burlesque Performance," *Brooklyn Daily Eagle*, February 3, 1906.
5. "Joke on Chairman Miller," *Brooklyn Daily Eagle*, February 2, 1906.
6. "Sympathy with Mr. Harding," *Brooklyn Daily Eagle*, February 9, 1906; "Case of Principal Harding," *Brooklyn Daily Eagle*, February 12, 1906.
7. "The Trial in Brownsville," *Yidishes Tageblatt*, January 31, 1906.

8. "The Case of Principal Harding," *Hebrew Standard*, March 16, 1906.
9. Albert Lucas, "Is a Jew Free and Equal before the Law," *American Hebrew and Jewish Messenger*, March 23, 1906.
10. "Very Unsatisfactory," *Hebrew Standard*, March 30, 1906; "Church and State," *American Hebrew and Jewish Messenger*, April 6, 1906.
11. Tobias Schanfarber, "News and Views," *American Israelite*, April 5, 1906.
12. "Principal Harding Wins," *Brooklyn Citizen*, March 27, 1906; "Charges against Harding Dismissed by Local Board," *Brooklyn Daily Eagle*, March 27, 1906; "Very Unsatisfactory"; "The Harding Case," *American Hebrew and Jewish Messenger*, April 13. 1906.

7. TO SAY THE LEAST, INDISCREET

1. "Church Conference On," *New York Tribune*, November 16, 1905.
2. Max Heller, "A Compromise," *American Israelite*, June 9, 1904; "Religion for the Schools," *New York Sun*, May 1, 1906; "Young Need Religion," *New York Tribune*, May 1, 1906.
3. "Religion for the Schools"; "Young Need Religion."
4. "Hands Off the Public Schools," *Hebrew Standard*, May 11, 1906.
5. "Religion in Schools," *Evening Star*, July 4, 1906.
6. David Kaufman, *Shul with a Pool: The "Synagogue-Center" in American Jewish History* (Waltham MA: Brandeis University Press, 1999), 142–43.
7. "The Beginning," *Hebrew Standard*, July 27, 1906.
8. "New York Happenings," *Reform Advocate*, April 7, 1906; "Jewish Centres Association," *Hebrew Standard*, September 28, 1906.
9. "The Harding Case," *American Hebrew and Jewish Messenger*, April 13, 1906; Jeffrey S. Gurock, "Why Albert Lucas Did Not Serve in the New York Kehillah," *Proceedings of the American Academy for Jewish Research* 51 (1984): 66.
10. "Bad Charter, Says Coles," *New York Sun*, April 9, 1901; "The Man in the Observatory," *Hebrew Standard*, October 28, 1904.
11. "Abraham Stern Dead," *New York Times*, July 3, 1927; *U.S. Passport Applications, 1795-1925*, Ancestry, accessed February 25, 2025, www.ancestry.com/search/collections/1174/records/979719; Hyman B. Grinstein, "The Efforts of East European Jewry to Organize Its Own Community in the United States," *Publications of the American Jewish Historical Society* 49, no. 2 (December 1959): 76; Gerald Sorin, "Mutual Contempt, Mutual Benefit: The Strained Encounter between German and Eastern European Jews in America, 1880–1920," *American Jewish History* 81, no. 1 (Autumn, 1993): 35–36; "Rodoph Sholom's New Officers Installed," *Hebrew Standard*, October 13, 1893.
12. "Principal Is Commended," *Brooklyn Daily Eagle*, January 31, 1906.
13. Minutes of the Board of Education Committee on Elementary Schools, January 23, 1906, and April 17, 1906, Records of the New York City Board of Education, series 137, New York City Department of Records/Municipal Archives, 26, 73.
14. Minutes of the Board of Education Committee on Elementary Schools, April 24, 1906, and May 22, 1906, Records of the New York City Board of Education, 77, 95.

15. "The Harding Case," *Hebrew Standard*, June 1, 1906; "The Harding Case Decision," *Hebrew Standard*, June 22, 1906.
16. Leonard Bloom, "A Successful Boycott of the New York City Public Schools—Christmas 1906," *American Jewish History* 70, no. 2 (December 1980): 183; Minutes of the Board of Education Committee on Elementary Schools, April 24, 1906, and May 29, 1906, Records of the New York City Board of Education, 77, 101–3.
17. "Can't Fully Exonerate Principal Harding," *Brooklyn Daily Eagle*, June 14, 1906; New York City Department of Education, *Journal of the Board of Education of the City of New York*, June 13, 1906: 941–51; Minutes of the Board of Education Committee on Elementary Schools, May 29, 1906, Records of the New York City Board of Education, 101–3.
18. New York City Department of Education, *Journal of the Board of Education of the City of New York*, 949–51.
19. "Boost for Salaries of School Officials," *Brooklyn Times*, June 14, 1906; "Ventilation Bad in 344 Schools," *Brooklyn Standard Union*, June 14, 1906; "Harding Case Decided," *American Hebrew and Jewish Messenger*, June 22, 1906; "Can't Fully Exonerate Principal Harding," *Brooklyn Daily Eagle*, June 14, 1906.
20. "The Missionary School Principal of Brownsville Is Declared Guilty," *Forverts*, June 15, 1906.
21. "The Harding Case Decision."

8. MURDERING OUR BABIES

1. Diane Ravitch, *The Great School Wars: New York City, 1805–1973* (New York: Basic Books, 1974), 167–68.
2. Luther Halsey Gulick and Leonard P. Ayres, *Medical Inspection of Schools* (New York: Survey Associates, 1913), 4, 13, 40, 63; "Emergency Hospital for Treatment of Trachoma," *New York Times*, January 25, 1903.
3. Gulick and Ayres, *Medical Inspection of Schools*, 81; Katherine Conroy and John Riddington Young, "A Brief History of Adenoidectomy—A Glowing Report of the Post Nasal Space," ENT and Audiology News, accessed April 21, 2023, www.entandaudiologynews.com/features/history-of-ent/post/a-brief-history-of-adenoidectomy-a-glowing-report-of-the-post-nasal-space.
4. "East Side Women Riot," *New York Tribune*, June 28, 1906.
5. "Crazed Women Storm Schools on East Side," *Brooklyn Times Union*, June 27, 1906; "Foolish Women," *Morgen Zhurnal*, June 28, 1906; John J. Cronin, "The Physical Defects of School Children," *Journal of the New York Institute of Stomatology* 2, no. 4 (December 1907): 280; Paul Theerman, "The Right to Health," New York Academy of Medicine Library Blog, accessed April 21, 2023, nyamcenterforhistory.org/tag/new-york-city-public-schools/#_ednref5.
6. "50,000 New York Jews Riot," *Chicago Tribune*, June 28, 1906; "Foolish Women"; "Residents of East Side Ready for Outbreak at Any Moment," *New York Tribune*, August 5, 1906.
7. "Foolish Women."

8. "East Side Parents Storm the Schools," *New York Times*, June 28, 1906.
9. "50,000 New York Jews Riot."
10. "Mob East Side Schools," *New York Post*, June 27, 1906; "50,000 New York Jews Riot"; "Residents of East Side Ready for Outbreak at Any Moment," *New York Tribune*, August 5, 1906.
11. "Residents of East Side Ready for Outbreak at Any Moment."
12. "Brownsville Imitates New York," *Yidishes Tageblatt*, June 29, 1906; "School Riots in Brownsville," *Morgen Zhurnal*, June 29, 1906.
13. "East Side Schools Mobbed by Hordes of Parents," *New York World*, June 27, 1906.
14. "Residents of East Side Ready for Outbreak at Any Moment"; Eddy Portnoy, "Sore," *Tablet*, August 19, 2010, accessed May 11, 2023, www.tabletmag.com/sections/community/articles/sore.
15. Myra Kelly, "Recent East Side Riots," *Colliers* 37, no. 27 (July 21, 1906): 15–16; Scott D. Seligman, *The Great Kosher Meat War of 1902: Immigrant Housewives and the Riots That Shook New York City* (Lincoln NE: Potomac Books, 2020).
16. "East Side Parents Storm the Schools," *New York Times*, June 28, 1906; "Panic Stricken Parents Mob East Side Schools," *Brooklyn Daily Eagle*, June 27, 1906; "Schools in Panic," *New York Sun*, June 28, 1906.
17. "Foolish Women"; "Brownsville Imitates New York."
18. "Residents of East Side Ready for Outbreak at Any Moment"; "Wild Mothers Mob East Side Schools," *New York Press*, June 28, 1906; "East Side Parents Storm the Schools."
19. "Schools in Panic," *New York Sun*, June 28, 1906.

9. NOTHING HARMFUL IN THESE OBSERVANCES

1. Donahoe v. Richards, 38 Me. 379 (1854); Moore v. Monroe, 64 Iowa 367 (1884).
2. Pfeiffer v. Board of Education, 118 Mich. 560 (1898); State ex rel. Weiss et al. v. District Board of School District No. 8 of the City of Edgerton, 76 Wis. 177 (1890).
3. Tobias Schanfarber and Samuel Hirshberg, eds., *Year Book of the Central Conference of American Rabbis*, vol. 16 (Cincinnati: Central Conference of American Rabbis, 1906), 164–65; Hackett v. Brooksville Graded School District, 120 Ky. 608 (1905).
4. "Won't Stand It," *Topeka State Journal*, December 17, 1901; "May Sue the School Board," *Evening Times Republican* (Marshalltown IA), December 18, 1901; "Religion in Public Schools," *Intermountain Catholic* (Salt Lake City UT), December 28, 1901; "That Bible Plan," *Topeka State Journal*, January 2, 1902; "Billard Gives Up," *Topeka State Journal*, January 4, 1902.
5. "The Bible as a Text Book in the Public Schools," *Blue-Grass Blade* (Lexington KY), August 24, 1902.
6. "Bible Barred from Schools," *Catoctin Clarion* (Thurmont MD), October 16, 1902; "Bars Bible from School," *Omaha Daily Bee*, October 10, 1902.
7. "Sectarianism in Public Schools," *Hebrew Standard*, October 12, 1906; "Rabbi I. L. Bril Dies, Editor and Writer," *New York Times*, March 3, 1936; *New Jersey School Laws, Revision*

of 1902 (Trenton NJ: John L. Murphy, 1902), 46–47; I. L. Brill, "Backbone, More Backbone," *Hebrew Standard*, October 12, 1906.

8. "Everywhere and Anywhere," *Hebrew Standard*, November 9, 1906.
9. Schanfarber and Hirshberg, *Year Book of the Central Conference of American Rabbis*, 151.
10. "School Board Enjoined by Jewess," *Buffalo Evening News*, July 1, 1906; "Examination of Teachers Held Up by the Court," *Buffalo Times*, July 1, 1906; "100 School Girls Indignant," *New York Sun*, July 2, 1906; "Justice Decides against Ms. Cohn," *Buffalo Evening News*, July 11, 1906; "Domestic," *Jewish Outlook*, July 21, 1906; "Cohn v. Townsend," Casetext, accessed January 28, 2023, casetext.com/case/cohn-v-townsend.
11. Central Conference of American Rabbis Committee on Church and State, *Why the Bible Should Not Be Read in the Public Schools* (n.p., 1906); "Rabbis Reject Synod Project," *Evening Star*, July 5, 1906; "American Rabbis Close Their Meeting," *Jewish Outlook*, July 13, 1906.
12. Schanfarber and Hirshberg, *Year Book of the Central Conference of American Rabbis*, 151–69.
13. Minutes of the Board of Education Committee on Elementary Schools, January 8, 1907, Records of the New York City Board of Education, series 137, New York City Department of Records/Municipal Archives, 3–4; "Jews Anti-Xmas Protest," *New York Times*, December 7, 1906. Rabbi Silverman denied the story about his daughter to the newspaper.
14. "Against Xmas," *Daily People*, December 6, 1906; "Don't Like Christmas," *New York Tribune*, December 6, 1906.
15. "Jews Anti-Xmas Protest."
16. "Don't Like Christmas."
17. "The Christmas Ceremonies in the Schools," *Morgen Zhurnal*, December 10, 1906.
18. "Christmas as Religious Day," *New York Telegram*, December 6, 1906.

10. EMPTY SEATS IN THE JEWISH NEIGHBORHOODS

1. "Xmas School Question Discussed in Letters," *New York Telegram*, December 11, 1906.
2. "Object to Observance of Xmas in Public Schools," *Brooklyn Times Union*, December 5, 1906.
3. "Struggle against Conversion Half Won," *Yidishes Tageblatt*, December 12, 1906. The words *ma yufis* begin verse 7:7 in the Song of Songs and refer to a dance that obsequious "court Jews" would perform for local landowners in order to gain favor. In a June 4, 2024, email to the author, University of California Yiddish professor emerita Yael Chaver characterized the epithet as the rough equivalent of the American expression, "Uncle Tom."
4. "Struggle against Conversion Half Won"; "The Protest before the School Board," *Die Wahrheit*, December 12, 1906.
5. "Struggle against Conversion Half Won"; "Protest before the School Board"; "Jewish Rabbis Protest," *New York Sun*, December 12, 1906; "May Report Today on Jews' Protests," *Brooklyn Standard Union*, December 12, 1906; "Board to Allow Xmas Observance in the

Schools," *New York Telegram,* December 12, 1906; "Methodist Pastors Appeal," *Brooklyn Daily Eagle,* December 13, 1906.

6. "Revolt of Jewish Pupils," *New York Sun,* December 24, 1906; "Against Xmas in Schools," *New York Times,* December 12, 1906; "Christmas in Public Schools," *Home Talk the Item,* December 19, 1906.
7. "Christmas in Public Schools."
8. "Communications," *American Hebrew and Jewish Messenger,* December 21, 1906.
9. "Anti-Christmas Strike," *New York Sun,* December 23, 1906; "Christmas Festival Opposed by Jews," *Evening Bulletin* (Providence RI), December 24, 1906.
10. "Don't Send Your Children to School on Monday," *Morgen Zhurnal,* December 23, 1906; "Tomorrow, Jewish Children Must Stop," *Yidishes Tageblatt,* December 23, 1906.
11. "Tomorrow, Jewish Children Must Stop."
12. "Don't Send Your Children to School on Monday"; "Tomorrow, Jewish Children Must Stop."
13. "Jewish Plan to Rebuke Xmas Day Services," *Brooklyn Daily Eagle,* December 23, 1906.
14. "Rabbis' Diverse Views," *New York Tribune,* December 24, 1906.
15. Judah Magnes, "The Jews and Christmas," *New York Post,* December 27, 1906.
16. "Hebrews of New York to Start School Strike," *Bay City* (TX) *Daily Tribune,* December 23, 1906; "Revolt of Jewish Pupils," *New York Sun,* December 24, 1906; "Jewish Plan to Rebuke Xmas Day Services."

11. THIS IS TOO MUCH TO ENDURE

1. "The Jewish Children Aren't Going to School Today," *Morgen Zhurnal,* December 24, 1906; "Christmas Boycott Urged," *New York Times,* December 23, 1906; "To Keep Children Out," *New York Tribune,* December 23, 1906; "Anti-Christmas Strike," *New York Sun,* December 23, 1906; "Jews Plan to Rebuke X-mas Day Services," *Brooklyn Daily Eagle,* December 23, 1906.
2. "Hebrew Pupils Out in Force at Xmas Season," *New York Telegram,* December 24, 1906; "Christmas in the Public Schools," *Jewish Outlook,* December 28, 1906.
3. "Jewish Pupils Absent for Xmas Exercises," *New York Times,* December 25, 1906.
4. "Boycott in Schools," *Die Wahrheit,* December 24, 1906; "Empty Schools," *Yidishes Tageblatt,* December 24, 1906; "The Schools Are Empty, Gone Are the Christmas Ceremonies," *Morgen Zhurnal,* December 25, 1906; "Religion in Schools Is Driven Away Forever," *Yidishes Tageblatt,* December 25, 1906.
5. "Jewish Pupils Absent for Xmas Exercises"; "Jewish Children Kept Away," *Omaha Daily Bee,* December 25, 1906; "Many Jews in School," *New York Tribune,* December 25, 1906.
6. "Jewish Pupils Absent for Xmas Exercises"; "New York Letter," *Plain Dealer,* January 9, 1907; "Religion in Schools Is Driven Away Forever."
7. "The Schools Are Empty, Gone Are the Christmas Ceremonies."
8. Editorial, *American Hebrew and Jewish Messenger,* December 28, 1906.
9. "The Schools Are Empty, Gone Are the Christmas Ceremonies"; "Empty Schools," *Yidishes Tageblatt,* December 24, 1906.

10. "Boycott in Schools," *Die Wahrheit*, December 24, 1906.
11. "Boycott in Schools"; "Jewish Pupils Absent for Xmas Exercises."
12. "Christmas in the Public Schools," *Jewish Outlook*, December 28, 1906.
13. "Many Jews in School," *New York Tribune*, December 25, 1906.
14. "Religion in Schools Is Driven Away Forever"; "The Boycott of Christmas," *Die Wahrheit*, December 25, 1906; "The Antisemites of Brownsville," *Die Wahrheit*, March 14, 1906.
15. "The Boycott of Christmas."
16. "Jews and Christmas," *Hebrew Standard*, December 28, 1906; "Jewish Pupils Absent for Xmas Exercises"; "Many Jews in School"; "Christmas in the Public Schools."
17. "Jewish Pupils Absent for Xmas Exercises"; Albert Lucas, "Christianity in Public Schools," *Hebrew Standard*, February 22, 1907.
18. "Jewish Pupils Absent for Xmas Exercises."
19. "Christ-Killing Jews in America," *Williamsport Republic*, December 27, 1906, as quoted in "Here Is the Result," *Jewish Voice*, January 11, 1907.
20. "Here Is the Result," *Jewish Voice*, January 11, 1907.
21. "Jewish Pupils Absent for Xmas Exercises," *New York Times*, December 25, 1906, quoting a statement from the editor of the *Yidishes Tageblatt*, December 25, 1906.
22. "Jewish Pupils Absent for Xmas Exercises"; "Mercury Drops a Bit," *New York Tribune*, December 24, 1906.
23. Jacob Riis, letter to Dr. Jane Robbins, December 26, 1906, as quoted in Jeffrey S. Gurock, "Jacob A. Riis: Christian Friend or Missionary Foe? Two Jewish Views," *American Jewish History* 71, no. 1 (September 1981), 46.
24. "The Jews and Public School Nonsectarianism," *Catholic Fortnightly Review* 14, no. 2 (January 5, 1907): 52–53; "Editorial Notes," *Jewish Voice*, January 25, 1907.
25. "Christmas without Christ," *Catholic Columbian*, December 29, 1906; "The Jews and Public School Nonsectarianism," 52–53.
26. "Christmas Exercises," *Jewish Outlook*, December 28, 1906.

12. SANCTIONED BY CUSTOM

1. *Journal of the Board of Education of the City of New York* (New York: Board of Education of the City of New York, 1907), 75–77.
2. "Compromise on Christmas," *Brooklyn Daily Eagle*, January 7, 1907; "School Compromise in Christmas Problem," *New York Times*, January 7, 1907.
3. Editorial, *American Hebrew and Jewish Messenger*, January 11, 1907.
4. "Jewish Leaders Say Faith Is in Danger," *New York Times*, January 10, 1907; "Union of American Hebrew Congregations," *Jewish Voice*, February 1, 1907.
5. "Twentieth Council of the Union of American Hebrew Congregations," *Jewish Voice*, January 25, 1907.
6. Albert Lucas, "Christianity in Public Schools," *Hebrew Standard*, February 22, 1907.
7. "Jewish Children against the Principal," *Die Wahrheit*, January 7, 1907; "Girls Defy the Principal," *Brooklyn Daily Eagle*, January 10, 1907; "Correspondence," *Jewish*

Outlook, January 18, 1907; "Brooklyn News," *American Hebrew and Jewish Messenger*, January 25, 1907.

8. "Jews Ask Clergymen to Attack Christmas," *Brooklyn Daily Eagle*, February 1, 1907.
9. "Jews Ask Clergymen to Attack Christmas."
10. Minutes of the Board of Education Committee on Elementary Schools, February 19, 1907, Records of the New York City Board of Education, series 137, New York City Department of Records/Municipal Archives; "Christmas Elimination to Be Topic at Meeting," *Brooklyn Daily Eagle*, November 27, 1907; *Journal of the Board of Education of the City of New York* (New York: Board of Education of the City of New York, 1907), 287–90; "No Christmas Carols in Schools This Year," *Brooklyn Daily Eagle*, November 21, 1907.
11. "Christmas Elimination to Be Topic at Meeting."
12. "Christmas Carols Protest," *New York Sun*, November 27, 1907; Rev. Louis Meyer, "Christianity in Our Public Schools and the Jews," *Christian Nation*, January 1, 1908; "Old Hymns and Christmas Stay in the Schools," *New York Herald*, November 28, 1907.
13. "Mr. Harding to Leave 144," *Brooklyn Daily Eagle*, June 13, 1907; "Award Contracts for New Schools," *Brooklyn Standard Union*, June 16, 1907; "Public School No. 144," *Brooklyn Daily Eagle*, June 27, 1907; "Brownsville Gets Rid of Principal Harding," *Yidishes Tageblatt*, September 5, 1907; "Correspondence," *Reform Advocate*, September 14, 1907.
14. "Orthodox Judaism," *Hebrew Standard*, June 21, 1907.
15. "New York Happenings," *American Israelite*, August 22, 1907; "The Opening of Public Schools," *Hebrew Standard*, August 16, 1907; "Want School Opening Postponed," *New York Tribune*, August 16, 1907; "For God and Faith," *Hebrew Standard*, August 16, 1907; "Editorial Notes," *Jewish News of Northern California*, August 30, 1907.
16. "Christmas Carols Barred," *New York Times*, November 21, 1907.

13. ANTI-SECTARIANISM HAS GONE MAD

1. "Wants Christmas Songs," *Brooklyn Daily Eagle*, November 22, 1907.
2. "More Heat Than Light in Protests over Carols," *Brooklyn Daily Eagle*, November 24, 1907.
3. "Hebrews on Education Board," *New York Tribune*, November 26, 1907; "A Maccabean Defense," *Hebrew Standard*, November 29, 1907; "Our New York Letter," *Reform Advocate*, November 30, 1907.
4. "Christmas without Christ," *Flint Journal*, November 23, 1907.
5. "Pressure Is Growing against School Board," *Brooklyn Daily Eagle*, November 25, 1907.
6. "What Catholics Seek for Parochial Schools," *Brooklyn Daily Eagle*, November 18, 1907; "Priest Attacks Jews," *New York Tribune*, December 6, 1907.
7. "Pulpits Laud and Score School Board's New Order," *New York Herald*, November 25, 1907.
8. "Board of Education Scored at Meetings," *Brooklyn Daily Eagle*, November 26, 1907.
9. "Board of Education Scored at Meetings."

10. "May Enjoin Education Board," *New York Sun,* November 25, 1907.
11. "School Christmas Ban Drives Rector to Law," *New York Press,* November 25, 1907; "Lindenmuller v. People," Casetext, accessed February 21, 2023, cite.case.law/barb/33/548/.
12. "School Christmas Ban Drives Rector to Law."
13. "Gen. Wingate on Xmas Exercises," *Brooklyn Standard Union,* November 26, 1907; "Christmas without Christ," *Catholic Standard,* November 30, 1907, as quoted in *Common Sense* (Union NJ), March 15, 1967.
14. "Board of Education Scored at Meetings," *Brooklyn Daily Eagle,* November 26, 1907.
15. "Christmas Elimination to Be Topic at Meeting," *Brooklyn Daily Eagle,* November 27, 1907; "Christmas Carols Protest," *New York Sun,* November 27, 1907.
16. "Allows Schools to Keep Christmas," *New York Times,* November 28, 1907.
17. "Christmas Dispute Up in Debate Today," *New York Times,* November 27, 1907; "War over Carols Teapot Tempest," *Chicago Tribune,* November 28, 1907; "Old Hymns and Christmas Stay in the Schools," *New York Herald,* November 28, 1907.
18. "Christian Clergy Protest Against New School Rule," *New York Herald,* November 26, 1907.
19. "May Hold Exercises," *New York Tribune,* November 28, 1907.
20. "Festivals Held in Public Schools," *New York Herald,* December 25, 1907.
21. "Correspondence," *Hebrew Standard,* February 28, 1908.
22. "The School Agitation," *Hebrew Standard,* December 6, 1907; "Will Keep Children Home," *Brooklyn Daily Eagle,* December 2, 1907.
23. "The School Agitation."

14. I WILL NOT BACK DOWN FROM THIS

1. Theodore A. Bingham, "Foreign Criminals in New York," *North American Review* 188, no. 634 (September 1908): 383, 385.
2. "The New Kehillah: Special Report," *Hebrew Standard,* March 5, 1909.
3. "The New Kehillah: Special Report"; "Our Weekly New York Bulletin," *Reform Advocate,* March 13, 1909.
4. Jeffrey S. Gurock, "Why Albert Lucas Did Not Serve in the New York Kehillah," *Proceedings of the American Academy for Jewish Research* 51 (1984): 55–72.
5. "Our New York Letter," *Reform Advocate,* December 7, 1907.
6. "Plans for the Kehillah's Bureau of Education," *Hebrew Standard,* October 7, 1910; "The Kehillah," *Hebrew Standard,* February 11, 1910; "Why Albert Lucas Did Not Serve in the New York Kehillah," 70.
7. "What the New York Kehillah Did during the Year," *American Hebrew and Jewish Messenger,* March 3, 1911.
8. The New Jersey statute was upheld by the Supreme Court in 1952 in the case of *Doremus v. Board of Education,* 342 U.S. 429 (1952); "Bible Bill Fails," *New York Times,* April 19, 1916.
9. "Devotional Exercises in Public Schools—Illegal," *Hebrew Standard,* October 2, 1908.

10. "Controversy Centers on Rev. C. E. Coughlin," *Waterbury* (CT) *Democrat*, December 12, 1938; "Priest Talks of Censure," *Quincy* (MA) *Patriot Ledger*, December 12, 1938.
11. "Brooklyn Schools Bar Nativity Carols; Inquiry Ordered," *Evening Star* (Washington DC), December 5, 1947; "Asks Probe of Brooklyn Ban on Yule Carols," *Daytona Beach* (FL) *Evening News*, December 5, 1947; "Brooklyn Pupils Denied Holiday Carols," *Huntsville* (AL) *Times*, December 5, 1947; "Clausen Sees Ban Misunderstood," *Brooklyn Daily Eagle*, December 5, 1947; "Ban on Christmas Carol Singing," *Providence* (RI) *Journal*, December 6, 1947; "Carol Ban Out of His Hands," *Brooklyn Daily Eagle*, December 8, 1947; "Bildersee Districts List Usual Yule Programs," *Brooklyn Daily Eagle*, December 14, 1947.

15. WE ACKNOWLEDGE OUR DEPENDENCE

1. Jonathan D. Sarna and David G. Dalin, *Religion and State in the American Jewish Experience* (Notre Dame IN: University of Notre Dame Press, 1997), 217.
2. "Daily Prayer in All Schools Is Urged by State's Regents," *New York Times*, December 1, 1951.
3. "Pastors Endorse School Prayers," *New York Times*, December 3, 1951; "Editor Backs Move for School Prayer," *New York Times*, December 14, 1951.
4. "School Prayer Fought," *New York Times*, December 10, 1951; "School Prayers Opposed," *New York Times* December 12, 1951.
5. "Two groups Decry Pupil Prayer Plan," *New York Times*, January 13, 1952.
6. "Rabbi Lauds Plan for School Prayer," *New York Times*, December 9, 1951; "Reform Rabbis Score School Prayers Plan," *New York Times*, December 15, 1951; "Regents Prayer Plan Is Opposed by Rabbis," *New York Times*, January 4, 1952.
7. "Regents Prayer Adopted Slowly," *New York Times*, October 12, 1952; "Prayer in School Still State Issue," *New York Times*, January 3, 1954.
8. "Free Thinker's Protest Bars Religion in School," *Jamestown Post-Journal*, June 14, 1945; "Religious Classes in Public Schools Closed by State," *Troy Times Record*, June 14, 1945; "School Periods for Religion End in 3 Towns," *Buffalo Courier-Express*, June 14, 1945; "Religious Education Ban Tested," *Rochester Times-Union*, June 15, 1945.
9. "School Pageants Upheld," *New York Times*, December 11, 1951.
10. "Atheist Likens School Pageant to Revival Program," *Kingston Daily Freeman*, December 20, 1950; "Atheist Cromwell Preparing Brief against Public School Religious Plays for State Body," *Syracuse Post-Standard*, December 21, 1950; "Atheist Hedges on Opposition to Yule Plays," *Salmanica Republican Press*, December 21, 1950.
11. "Yule in School Critic Receives Protest Notes," *Rochester Democrat and Chronicle*, December 22, 1950.
12. "Clergyman Hits Back at Foe of Pageants," *Lockport Union-Sun*, December 21, 1950.
13. "Atheist Likens School Pageant to Revival Program," *Kingston Daily Freeman*, December 20, 1950; "Contends Pageants 'Little Different' Than Act of Thief," *Evening Leader and Corning Democrat*, December 22, 1950; "Wilson Refuses to Ban Religious Plays in Schools," *Knickerbocker News*, December 11, 1951; "School Pageants Upheld," *New York Times*, December 11, 1951.

14. "School Religion Draws Protests," *New York Times*, July 26, 1958.
15. "Fight over Christmas in Schools Flares into Anti-Semitic Cross Burnings," *National Jewish Post and Opinion*, April 26, 1957.
16. "Crèche Case Arguments Are Delayed," *Utica Observer-Dispatch*, December 12, 1957; "Protest against Nativity Scene Called 'Nonsense'," *Tablet*, December 21, 1957; "The Christmas Spirit," *Birmingham Post-Herald*, December 17, 1957; "Crèche at School Upheld by Court," *New York Times*, December 21, 1957.
17. "Jews Protesting L.I. School Policy," *New York Times*, November 27, 1958; "Ban on Discussion of Chanukah in Public Schools Evokes Protests," *Jewish Telegraphic Agency*, November 28, 1958.
18. "Schools of New Hyde Park to Show Ten Commandments," *Long Islander*, November 29, 1956; "School District Ordered Not to Post Commandments," *Ogdensburg* (NY) *Journal*, June 12, 1957; "N.Y. Commissioner of Education Bans 'Public School Ten Commandments'," Jewish Telegraphic Agency, June 14, 1947; "Ban Asked on Decalogue," *Catholic Courier Journal*, December 28, 1956.
19. David L. Hudson Jr., "Engel v. Vitale (1962)," First Amendment Encyclopedia, accessed April 26, 2023, www.mtsu.edu/first-amendment/article/665/engel-v-vitale; "School District of Abington Township, Pennsylvania v. Schempp," Oyez, accessed April 26, 2023, www.oyez.org/cases/1962/142; "The Law," *New York Times*, December 29, 1965.
20. "Abington School District v. Schempp," 374 U.S. 203 (1963), Justia, accessed September 7, 2023, supreme.justia.com/cases/federal/us/374/203/#tab-opinion-1944457.
21. "Lemon v. Kurtzman," Oyez, accessed May 7, 2024, www.oyez.org/cases/1970/89; "Kennedy v. Bremerton School District," Casetext, accessed May 7, 2024, casetext.com /case/kennedy-v-bremerton-school-dist-1.
22. "County of Allegheny v. American Civil Liberties Union," Oyez, accessed June 23, 2024, www.oyez.org/cases/1988/87-2050; Charles J. Russo and Ralph D. Mawdsley, "Legal Issues Surrounding Christmas in Public Schools," *Educational Leadership Faculty Publications*, 174; "Lynch v. Donnelly (1984)," National Constitution, accessed June 7, 2024, constitutioncenter.org/the-constitution/supreme-court-case-library/lynch-v-donnelly.
23. "Lawsuit Attacks Schools' Ban on Nativity Scenes," *New York Times*, December 11, 2002.
24. "Skoros v. City of New York, 437 F. 3d 1—Court of Appeals, 2nd Circuit 2006," Google Scholar, accessed May 20, 2023, scholar.google.com/scholar_case?case= 11069334439388113731; "Nativity Scene Is Too Religious for New York City Schools," *Christian Science Monitor*, February 22, 2007.

16. NOT YET LEARNED HOW TO WAGE WAR

1. "Our New York Letter," *Reform Advocate*, December 7, 1907.
2. "Board of Education Scored at Meetings," *Brooklyn Daily Eagle*, November 26, 1907.
3. Stuart Banner, "When Christianity Was Part of the Common Law," *Law and History Review* 16, no. 1 (Spring 1998): 27–62.
4. "Christian Hymns in Public Schools," *American Hebrew and Jewish Messenger*, December 25, 1903; "Christmas in Public Schools," *American Hebrew and Jewish Messenger*, December 29, 1905.

5. Jonathan D. Sarna and David G. Dalin, *Religion and State in the American Jewish Experience* (Notre Dame IN: University of Notre Dame Press, 1997), 203–8.
6. "McCollum v. Board of Education, 333 U.S. 203 (1948)," Justia, accessed September 30, 2023, supreme.justia.com/cases/federal/us/333/203/; "Zorach v. Clauson, 343 U.S. 306 (1952)," Findlaw, accessed May 19, 2023, caselaw.findlaw.com/court/us-supreme-court/343/306.html; "For a Lot of American Teens, Religion Is a Regular Part of the Public School Day," Pew Research Center, accessed May 19, 2023, www.pewresearch.org/religion/2019/10/03/for-a-lot-of-american-teens-religion-is-a-regular-part-of-the-public-school-day/.
7. "Issue of Christmas in Public Schools," *National Jewish Post and Opinion*, December 17, 1965; "Most U.S. Public Schools Ignore Laws against Prayer," *Sentinel*, June 24, 1976; "74% of Americans Say Christmas Should Be Celebrated in Public Schools," *Washington Times*, December 11, 2018.

AFTERWORD

1. "Dealing with the Christmas Observance in the Public Schools," *American Jewish Committee*, October 23, 1956.
2. Leonard Gross, "The Jew and Christmas," *Look*, December 28, 1965.
3. "The (November and) December Dilemma: Holiday Guidelines for Public Schools and Public Spaces," Anti-Defamation League, accessed May 5, 2023, lasvegas.adl.org/december-dilemma-holiday-guidelines-for-public-schools-and-public-spaces/.
4. Jonathan D. Sarna, "Is Judaism Compatible with American Civil Religion?" in Rowland A. Sherrill, ed., *Religion in the Life of the Nation* (Urbana: University of Illinois Press, 1990), 160; "Jewish Congress Warns on Chanukah and Christmas Observances in Schools," December 13, 1965, Jewish Telegraphic Agency, accessed June 14, 2024, www.jta.org/archive/jewish-congress-warns-on-chanukah-and-christmas-observances-in-schools; Ronald Kahn, "Judaism," Middle Tennessee State University Free Speech Center, accessed October 10, 2024, firstamendment.mtsu.edu/article/judaism/; John R. Vile, "Leo Pfeffer," Middle Tennessee State University Free Speech Center, accessed October 10, 2024, firstamendment.mtsu.edu/article/leo-pfeffer/.
5. "Jewish Americans in 2020," Pew Research Center, accessed May 12, 2023, www.pewresearch.org/religion/2021/05/11/jewish-identity-and-belief/ and www.pewresearch.org/religion/2021/05/11/marriage-families-and-children/.
6. "How U.S. Religious Composition Has Changed in Recent Decades," Pew Research Center, accessed May 13, 2023, www.pewresearch.org/religion/2022/09/13/how-u-s-religious-composition-has-changed-in-recent-decades/; Kelefa Sanneh, "How Christian Is Christian Nationalism?" *New Yorker*, March 27, 2023.
7. "Unlicensed Religious Chaplains May Counsel Students in Texas' Public Schools after Lawmakers OK Proposal," May 24, 2023, *Texas Tribune*, accessed June 11, 2023, www.texastribune.org/2023/05/24/texas-legislature-chaplains-schools/; "Is Prayer Coming Back to Public Schools?" April 12, 2023, Public School Review, accessed June 11, 2023, www.publicschoolreview.com/blog/is-prayer-coming-back-to-public-schools; "No Christian Proselytization to Schoolchildren, FFRF Warns Arkansas School District,"

May 16, 2023, Freedom from Religion Foundation, accessed June 11, 2023, ffrf.org/news/news-releases/item/42250-no-christian-proselytization-to-schoolchildren-ffrf-warns-arkansas-school-district; "Oklahoma Approves First Religious Charter School in the U.S.," *New York Times*, June 5, 2023.

8. "Carson v. Makin," Casetext, accessed May 7, 2023, casetext.com/case/carson-v-makin-5/; "Kennedy v. Bremerton School District," Casetext Website, accessed May 7, 2023, https://casetext.com/case/kennedy-v-bremerton-school-dist-1.
9. "Louisiana Requires Ten Commandments to Be Displayed in Public Classrooms," *Washington Post*, June 20, 2024; "Stone v. Graham," Casetext, accessed July 19, 2024, casetext.com/case/stone-v-graham; "Lemon v. Kurtzman," Oyez, accessed May 7, 2024, www.oyez.org/cases/1970/89.
10. "Americans Say Religious Aspects of Christmas Are Declining in Public Life," Pew Research Center, accessed May 13, 2023, www.pewresearch.org/religion/2017/12/12/americans-say-religious-aspects-of-christmas-are-declining-in-public-life/.
11. "Alito's 'Godliness' Comment Echoes a Broader Christian Movement," *New York Times*, June 11, 2024.
12. "Fact Check: Trump's Pledge to Restore 'Merry Christmas' to the White House," NPR, November 30, 2017, accessed May 28, 2023, www.npr.org/2017/11/30/567525913/fact-check-trump-s-pledge-to-restore-merry-christmas-to-the-white-house; Merry Christmas Texas website, accessed November 20, 2023, merrychristmastexas.com/christmas-bill-summary.pdf.
13. "45% of Americans Say U.S. Should Be a 'Christian Nation,'" Pew Research Center, accessed May 11, 2023, www.pewresearch.org/religion/2022/10/27/45-of-americans-say-u-s-should-be-a-christian-nation/.
14. "Americans Say Religious Aspects of Christmas Are Declining in Public Life."

Index